LITERARY/CULTURAL THEORY

SUBALTERN STUDIES

Literary/Cultural Theory provides concise and lucid introductions to a range of key concepts and theorists in contemporary literary and cultural theory. Original and contemporary in presentation, and eschewing jargon, each book in the series presents students of humanities and social sciences exhaustive overviews of theories and theorists, while also introducing them to the mechanics of reading literary/cultural texts using critical tools. Each book also carries glossaries of key terms and ideas, and pointers for further reading and research. Written by scholar-teachers who have taught critical theory for years, and vetted by some of the foremost experts in the field, the series Literary/Cultural Theory is indispensable to students and teachers.

Series Editors

Allen Hibbard
Middle Tennessee State University

Andrew Slade
University of Dayton

Herman Rapaport
Wake Forest University

Imre Szeman
University of Alberta

Krishna Sen
University of Calcutta

Scott Slovic
University of Idaho

Sumit Chakrabarti
Presidency University, Kolkata

Also in the series

Psychoanalytic Theory and Criticism
Feminisms
Jacques Lacan
Dalit Literature and Criticism
Ecocriticism
Postcolonialism Now
Marxist Literary and Cultural Theory
Postsecular Theory
Nations and Nationalisms
Periyar
Popular Culture
Queer Studies
Frantz Fanon
Mikhail Bakhtin
Deconstruction and Poststructuralism
Edward Said
Diaspora Theory and Transnationalism
Life Writing

LITERARY/CULTURAL THEORY

SUBALTERN STUDIES
A SHORT INTRODUCTION

GARGI TALAPATRA

The Bhawanipur Education Society College, Kolkata

Edited by
Krishna Sen

University of Calcutta

Orient BlackSwan

All rights reserved. No part of this book may be modified, reproduced or utilised in any form, or by any means, electronic or mechanical, including photocopying, recording or by any information storage and retrieval system, in any form of binding or cover other than in which it is published, without permission in writing from the publisher.

SUBALTERN STUDIES: A SHORT INTRODUCTION

ORIENT BLACKSWAN PRIVATE LIMITED

Registered Office
3-6-752 Himayatnagar, Hyderabad 500 029, Telangana, India
Email: centraloffice@orientblackswan.com

Other Offices
Bengaluru, Chennai, Guwahati, Hyderabad, Kolkata, Mumbai, New Delhi, Noida, Patna

© Orient Blackswan Private Limited 2024
First published 2024

ISBN 978 93 5442 657 5

Typeset in Aldine 401 BT 10.5/13 *by*
Akhil Offset Printers
Hyderabad 500 020

Printed at
Shree Maitrey Printech Pvt. Ltd., Noida.

Published by
Orient Blackswan Private Limited
3-6-752, Himayatnagar,
Hyderabad 500 029, Telangana, India
Email: info@orientblackswan.com

039201

The publisher has endeavoured to ensure that the URLs for external websites referred to in this book are correct and active at the time of going to press. However, the publisher has no responsibility for the websites and can make no guarantee that a site will remain live or that the content is or will remain appropriate.

*Dedicated to my grandfather,
the Late Sri Paritosh Kumar Pain*

Contents

Editor's Preface	*ix*
Acknowledgements	*xiii*
Introduction	*xv*
1. Subaltern Studies: The Theoretical Perspective	1
2. The Subaltern Studies Collective	19
3. Subaltern Studies and Postcolonialism	37
4. Subaltern Studies and Postcolonial Feminism *The Gendered Subaltern*	55
5. Subaltern Studies and the Dalit Experience	83
6. Subaltern Studies in Latin America	108
7. Subalternity and Disability Studies	125
8. Extending the Boundaries *Borderlands and Multiple Worlds*	142
9. Reading Subalternity in Films	163
Glossary of Select Terms	*178*
Further Reading	*181*

Editor's Preface

It gives me great pleasure to write the Editor's Preface for Gargi Talapatra's *Subaltern Studies*, which forms part of Orient BlackSwan's *Literary/Cultural Theory* series. A major highlight of this monograph is that it is one of the very few comprehensive and critical studies of this major theoretical paradigm. Fittingly, since this is a theory that was first conceptualised in India by Indian scholars and historians led by the late Ranajit Guha, the entire discussion (except for the chapter on Latin American Subaltern Studies) is grounded in Indian literary and cultural formations which offer significant insights into the Indian contexts, which is a major contribution of this volume.

Talapatra begins by distinguishing between the Western and Indian concepts of the subaltern. Gramsci's iconic coinage of the term 'subaltern' to denote both marginalisation and exploitation in his *Prison Notebooks* was reconfigured by Eric Hobsbawm to denote what he called a 'pre-political' identity. The Indian Subaltern Studies Collective has rejected the interpretation of the subaltern as 'pre-political' as being both misconstrued and elitist. Through his exhaustive analysis of colonial peasant uprisings in India, Ranajit Guha shows, on the contrary, how the peasant and tribal consciousness manifested in these rebellions was intensely political. He further argues that this subaltern political consciousness can be reconstructed by exploring the gaps and fissures in the dominant narratives of mainstream historians. To amplify this line of thought, Talapatra offers a detailed discussion of the major perspectives of the Subaltern Studies Collective as reflected in the twelve volumes of its signature publication, *Subaltern Studies*.

Another important contribution of the present monograph is its careful and critical delineation of the way in which Subaltern Studies theorisation in India complicated its initial Marxist and Foucauldian thrust with the introduction of postcolonial perspectives by theorists like Dipesh Chakrabarty and novelists like Salman Rushdie in *Midnight's Children* and Arundhati Roy in *The God of Small Things*.

We have, therefore, seen that the Indian theorisation of the subaltern as explicated in Subaltern Studies theory differs notably from Western interpretations of social marginalisation. The subaltern figure in India is highly politically conscious, rather than 'pre-political', and the strategies of power that s/he contends with are problematised by issues of postcoloniality.

A major marker that sets the Indian subaltern apart from his/her class-based Western counterpart is the exclusively Indian dimension of caste. Talapatra engages in a detailed discussion of the Dalit subaltern. She offers us the stages in the evolution of a Dalit consciousness in India – the caste-based hierarchies of Indian society as recorded by colonial British historians, the concurrent sociological construction of caste by scholars such as G. S. Ghurye in the 1930s and 40s, the emergence of a singular Dalit identity under leaders like B. R. Ambedkar, the foregrounding of Dalit nationalism and its close ties with the American Black Panther Movement in the 1970s, and finally, the articulation of a nationalist Dalit aesthetics by Dalit intellectuals like Sharankumar Limbale. This section concludes with close readings of selected Dalit fiction and autobiographies, whose lineage has been traced back to the 'lower-caste' poets of the Bhakti Movement of the twelfth century such as Eknath and Chokhamela.

The discussion also focuses subaltern concerns in feminist theory by looking, first at African American Womanism and then at Gayatri Chakravorty Spivak's interventions beginning from the fourth volume of *Subaltern Studies*. Here, Spivak offered a gendered reading of the doubly marginalised position of the subaltern woman-figure, followed subsequently in the fifth volume by a translation of Mahasweta Devi's short story, *Stanadayini* ('Breast-Giver'). These insights were later developed by Spivak in her seminal essay, 'Can the Subaltern Speak?'. The section moves on to discuss the Dalit feminist writings of Bama, Meena Kandasamy and *Dalit Lekhika* (2020) edited by Kalyani Thakur Charal and Sayantan Dasgupta.

In addition, this volume calls attention to an important extension in the Indian discourse of Subaltern Studies that goes beyond the trajectory of the original Subaltern Studies Collective – the interface of Disability Studies and Subaltern Studies within the interdisciplinary narrative developed by Anita Ghai, first in her essay 'Engaging with

Disability with Postcolonial Theory' (2012) where she asks 'whether the Subaltern (read disabled) can speak'. To illustrate this new facet in Subaltern Studies, this book provides critical readings of the representation of marginalisation of disability in fiction by Amitav Ghosh, Salman Rushdie and Anita Desai, as well as autobiographies ranging from that of Helen Keller to the narrative by Malini Chib.

The range and depth of the present study may be seen in the other chapters as well. There is an extensive discussion of Subaltern Studies as theorised in Latin America and represented in its literature. Further, in separate chapters, the discussion also engages with the portrayal of the subaltern in Bollywood movies and the position of the subaltern in 'borderland' locations such as Kashmir, North-east India, the *chhitmahals* of the Indo-Bangladesh border and Latin America.

In its wide-ranging scope, clarity of presentation, well-developed arguments and copious illustrations from the Indian context, this volume is an important contribution to the discursive analysis of Subaltern Studies. In the course of her discussion, Gargi Talapatra simultaneously defines, analyses and problematises several issues relating to the position of the subaltern. This lucid and informative monograph will, therefore, be of interest both to the general reader and to students and researchers.

Krishna Sen

Acknowledgements

Every book that sees the light of day has stories behind its coming into being. This book is no different. While I put these words on paper, the book was continuously nurtured by people around me. Without their constant support and encouragement, the book would not have been possible.

It was beyond me to think that I could go through the process of writing a book on Subaltern Studies, and it would not have been possible without the guidance, inspiration and encouragement of my teacher, Professor Krishna Sen, who introduced me to Subaltern Studies as a student and whose faith in my abilities stood firm throughout these years. Her insights and observations have enriched me and enabled me to grasp the nuances. I am deeply grateful to her for giving me this opportunity.

I would like to thank my teachers and mentors, Barnali Pain and Indrajit Chaudhuri, for the resources and the innumerable exciting discussions on the subject which resulted in the exploration of several new angles associated with Subaltern Studies. Without their constant intellectual and emotional support, this journey would not have been possible.

I extend my heartfelt thanks to Manimanjari Mitra, a senior scholar of history and a close friend, for providing me with interesting inputs as I waded my way through the multiple manifestations of subalternity.

Without the peace of a secure space, thoughts cannot acquire a coherent language. I am thankful to my parents, Supriya Talapatra and Rinku Talapatra, for providing me with constant support in my academic endeavours.

No speculations on a subject can assume a concrete shape without the life that the classroom space breathes into it. My students have been instrumental in adding to my enthusiasm about the book with their intellectual curiosity and lively discussions.

I would also like to thank my department and my friends for the multiple sessions of stimulating conversations which resulted in renewed perspectives.

Finally, I owe my thanks to Orient BlackSwan for initiating the *Literary/Cultural Theory* series and including me as a part of this wonderful initiative to promote academic and critical thinking and research.

Introduction

As the world was hit by COVID-19 and struggled to cope with the pandemic, a major part of news in the 'new normal' era of online interactions was about the miserable plight of migrant workers. When the first round of lockdown was announced by the Government of India, on 24 March 2020, a large number of migrant workers were left stranded in alien cities without work, food or money. The measures to contain the pandemic, such as wearing masks, staying indoors, practising social distancing and strengthening the immune system through proper diet, were, unfortunately, all essentially elitist. These measures relied on ready provision of basic survival requirements, and did not apply to this section of subaltern population which has been the major driving force behind urban economies and yet remains largely invisible under 'normal' circumstances. This invisibility is deliberately constituted by the mainstream majority, through a habitual thoughtlessness of the privileged, and is one of the major characteristics defining subalternity.

In other words, the term 'subaltern' refers to the section of the population whose presence is overlooked by the mainstream society and remains undocumented by official histories. They are marginalised and their voices remain unheard. Antonio Gramsci, in his *Prison Notebooks* (1971), defines the 'subaltern' as those who are not unified and cannot unite. Historically, they remain voiceless as the official archives do not record their utterances. According to Gramsci, these subaltern groups are subjected to ideological influences through hegemonic practices by the dominant groups. This leads to an osmotic interaction and results in continuous changes in the texture and composition of the subaltern groups. Subalternity as a marker of identity is, therefore, not determined through uniform parameters. While the term refers to people who are marginalised by social, historical and political structures of power – implying the poor and vulnerable sections of the population – unlike the European understanding of the subaltern as the poor or the worker, based on class identities, the Asian, and particularly Indian, qualifiers of subalternity are much more varied and complex. Cutting across the markers of identity such as race, caste, gender as well as ethnicity, the identification of the subaltern in the Indian context leads to the recognition of a more complex matrix of subalternity. It is so because subalternity in India is not unidimensional – more than one parameter may be operative in the paradigm of the Indian subaltern. The first chapter traces this departure of the concept of subalternity from the European sense of the term, and relocates it in the context of India through theorisations found in Frantz Fanon's *The Wretched of the Earth* (1961) and Edward Said's *Orientalism* (1978), locating the subaltern as a postcolonial subject. It provides an overview of the emergence of the Subaltern Studies Group in India – founded by Ranajit Guha – and distinguishes the Indian understanding of the subaltern from the Western connotations associated with it by Marxist scholars and historians like E. J. Hobsbawm who identified the subaltern population as 'pre-political' in his seminal work, *Primitive Rebels* (1959). The chapter also looks at the formation of the Subaltern Studies Group in Latin America in the 1990s by scholars and historians like John Beverley and Ileana Rodríguez, following the vision of the Indian collective.

The formation of the Subaltern Studies Collective in India led by scholars and historians like Ranajit Guha, Gautam Bhadra, Sumit Sarkar, Tanika Sarkar, Partha Chatterjee, Dipesh Chakrabarty and Gyanendra Pandey, and later, Gayatri Chakravorty Spivak who brought in the question of the gendered subaltern, resulted in an exploration of the heterogeneity of subaltern uprisings and voices – which are lost to the mainstream archives of history – through a collection of twelve volumes titled *Subaltern Studies*, published by the group from 1982 to 2005. The second chapter retraces these perspectives introduced by the Subaltern Studies Collective in locating subaltern utterances. Beginning with the subaltern insurgencies in Mughal India and the 1857 Uprising, the chapter explores how the Collective provided detailed explorations of the conditions of the Calcutta Jute Mill Workers, the role of the subaltern population in the twentieth-century nationalist movements, and narratives of insurgencies in Adivasi politics, and gradually expanded its vision to include within the scope of Subaltern Studies questions of nation, gender, caste, religion and diaspora. Narrating the disintegration of the Collective in the late 1990s, the chapter investigates the relevance of Subaltern Studies in the present times with reference to Vivek Chibber's *Postcolonial Theory and the Spectre of Capital* (2013). The third chapter differentiates between two concepts – the idea of a people's history advocated by British historians like E. P. Thompson through the concept of 'history from below', and the approach adopted by Subaltern Studies in the postcolonial context. This chapter provides an overview of the trajectory of Subaltern Studies with reference to postcolonialism, and shows how despite Marxist and Foucauldian understandings of power which brings Subaltern Studies close to the idea of 'history from below', it goes beyond it in its scope by becoming a practice of reading postcolonial history against the grain. The chapter, further, analyses representations of subalternity in postcolonial literature with reference to select works of Salman Rushdie and Arundhati Roy.

While postcolonial subjectivity problematises the identity of the subaltern, 'gender' introduces a different complexity into the theoretical considerations around the subaltern. The fourth chapter explores the existence and representations of the gendered subaltern. It identifies the limitations of the First and Second Wave feminisms and traces the gradual emergence of feminism as a plural concept with reference to African American feminism and postcolonial feminism – which expanded the scope of feminism to include caste and community within the discourse of subalternity. The chapter goes back to Gayatri Chakravorty Spivak's essay 'Can the Subaltern Speak?' (1988) and Chandra Talpade Mohanty's 'Under Western Eyes: Feminist Scholarship and Colonial Discourses' (1987). It also explores Dalit feminism as a specific form of Postcolonial feminism. It further engages in detailed analyses of important works by Toni Morrison, Alice Walker, Mahasweta Devi, Bama and Meena Kandasamy, to illustrate the doubly subjugated identity of the woman as the gendered subaltern.

Of the markers of identity associated with the identification of the subaltern in the Indian context, caste, perhaps, has been the most complex. The idea of transcending caste hierarchies has been a crucial theme in the history of India since the Bhakti movement, dating back to the twelfth century. During the colonial era, the concept of caste became perhaps the most complex issue for the colonisers to deal with in India – for while caste in the social fabric of India may be subdivided into *'jaati'* and *'varna'*, which further branches out into several subdivisions, to the West it implied race, lineage or tribe. Accordingly, several attempts at a caste-based stratification of the society were made by historians like John Watson and John Kaye, in *The People of India*, and later by ethnographers like Herbert Risley. The latter half of the twentieth century, similarly, saw several volumes exploring the sociological perspectives of caste by writers such as G. S. Ghurye, Louis Dumont and M. N. Srinivas. The fifth chapter is devoted to the study of caste as a component of subalternity. It maps the presence of caste as a political and social consciousness in the Indian society, and traces the gradual evolution of Dalit consciousness and Dalit nationalism with reference to Periyar, B. R. Ambedkar and V. T. Rajshekar. The chapter also provides a detailed analysis of Dalit writings in the form of fiction and autobiographies across different regions of India, while touching upon the question of Dalit aesthetics as addressed by writers like Imayam and theorists like Sharankumar Limbale.

The sixth chapter looks at the emergence of the Latin American Subaltern Studies Group in 1993, and traces its socio-political background across the Mexican, Cuban and Nicaraguan revolutions which necessitated a departure from the erstwhile perspectives adopted by Latin American Studies and Latin American Boom evolving in the 1960s. It provides an analysis of subalternity in Latin American literatures through close readings of select works of Gabriel García Márquez and Rigoberta Menchú.

Subalternity is marked by exploitation and denial of basic rights. In the present context of a mainstream 'ableist' society – where everyday life and even use of language is governed by a widespread tendency towards exclusion – one of the most significant markers constituting subalternity is 'disability'. This is a more recent extension of subalternity – a fresh turn which extends beyond the Subaltern Studies movement. It finds expression in Anita Ghai's 'Engaging with Disability with Postcolonial Theory' where she reiterates Spivak's famous question as – 'whether the Subaltern (read disabled) can Speak?' The seventh chapter, therefore, provides an overview of Disability Rights movements and theorises

Disability Studies as an aspect of Subaltern Studies. It explores the subaltern subjectivity through representations of disability in Indian myths and select literary works. The chapter critiques disability as represented in Amitav Ghosh's *Circle of Reason*, Salman Rushdie's *Midnight's Children* and Anita Desai's *Clear Light of Day*. It also analyses disability as represented in the subjective experiences of Helen Keller, Nick Vujicic, Malini Chib and Preeti Monga.

The eighth chapter explores subalternity in terms of spatial demarcations. Postcolonialism, with the passage of time, has led to the emergence of several strands of nationalisms and subnationalisms. While there are specific cartographic lines which bestow a specific national citizenship on an individual, the gradual emergence of multiple world orders and the problematised existence of 'borderlands' raise significant questions, as statist apparatuses impose ethnic homogenisation or historical reimaginings on the inhabitants of the borderlands. This chapter includes an exploration of subalternity as constituted by literatures associated with borderlands. It includes studies of literary representations of lives in the Indo-Bangladesh Conclaves (also known as the *chhitmahal*), the ridges, North-east India, Kashmir and Latin America.

A discussion of representations of subalternity in the present times is incomplete without referring to films and cinematic representations, since they constitute the most popular form of audiovisual mass entertainment and play a significant role in shaping social response. The last chapter attempts to analyse representations of class, caste, gender and disability-based subalternity in select films, to trace the trajectory of popular discourse as formulated by Hindi films. The decision to discuss 'Bollywood' films was taken consciously, since it dominates mainstream discourses, and has an important role to play in agenda-setting and formation of dominant discourses. The chapter also analyses how most of these films leave out uncomfortable narratives of social injustices and subalternisation. The films critiqued in this chapter include *Bazaar* (1982), *Aakrosh* (1980), *Koshish* (1972), *Rudaali* (1993), *Mangal Pandey* (2005), *Article 15* (2019) and *Bulbbul* (2020).

Considering the wide scope of the subject, this introduction to Subaltern Studies does not claim to be an exhaustive analysis of all forms or works concerning subalternity. It attempts to provide readers and researchers with the basic tools to comprehend the multiple manifestations of subalternity that lie latent in our society, as an integral part of everyday lives and existence.

REFERENCES

Fanon, Frantz. *The Wretched of the Earth*. 1961. Penguin, 1967.

Ghai, Anita. 'Engaging with Disability with Postcolonial Theory'. *Disability and Social Theory: New Developments and Directions*. Ed. Dan Goodley, Bill Hughes and Lennard Davis. Palgrave Macmillan, 2012. 270–86.

Gramsci, Antonio. *Selections from the Prison Notebooks*. International Publishers, 1971.

Hobsbawm, E. J. *Primitive Rebels*. <https://www.scribd.com/doc/310782738/eric-hobsbawm-primitive-rebels-pdf#download>.

Said, Edward. *Orientalism*. Pantheon, 1978.

Spivak, Gayatri Chakravorty. 'Can the Subaltern Speak?'. *Literary Theory: An Introductory Reader*. Ed. Saugata Bhaduri and Simi Malhotra. Anthem Press, 2010. 263–318.

Chapter One

Subaltern Studies: The Theoretical Perspective

Alternative voices, marginalised and suppressed by dominant power structures in society, have always found their expression in literature. Latent in the apparent historical progress of society, alternative voices have continued to exist since ancient times in the form of oral or folk literature. However, mostly undocumented, these utterances are often lost through the cracks of time. These expressions vary from community to community and region to region, and acquire various forms. In 'Traditions of folk in Literature', Indranath Choudhuri writes that these traditions of alternative voices have been assimilated in what is understood as *loka*, and observes: 'the *loka* (folk) and *shastra* (elite) are complementary' (4). In the Indian context, these two streams taken together enable us to understand the expanse and diversity of the Indian aesthetic and discursive traditions.

However, this classification of the 'subaltern' (a more detailed definition of which we will arrive at in the following section) is not confined to the Indian context alone. Such expressions of alternative suppressed voices have similarly been felt in societies across the world from time to time. Just as one finds Chokhamela and Eknath in the Indian context in fourteenth-century Marathi poetry representing the medieval lower castes, one encounters the subjugated utterances in the American slave narratives of the eighteenth and nineteenth centuries. Since the experience of oppression cannot be dated to any particular point of time in history, alternative voices and modes of narration documenting oppression cannot be restricted to a specific geospatial world order. Writers and theorists have often focused on unearthing the forgotten voices of the oppressed. For instance, George Manuel and Michael Posluns' *The Fourth World: An Indian Reality* (1974), focusing on the indigenous peoples and communities and their right to self-determination, launched the Four Worlds theory – the Fourth World comprising the marginalised of the First, Second and Third worlds. But Subaltern Studies as a discipline was the first to recognise the wider sociopolitical implications of this concept, and to give it a theoretical grounding from a Marxist perspective.

THE TERM AND THE CONCEPT

The term 'subaltern' refers to those sections of society whose voices, actions and presence have been overlooked by mainstream documentation of official histories. These subaltern utterances do not contribute to mainstream discourses and therefore, are marginalised by official historiography. For instance, in the context of nations and nationalisms, the mainstream documents often record dominant aspects of elitist nationalism and nationalist movements, while the contribution of marginalised indigenous people and communities is consigned to the peripheries. In the process, these utterances are lost and overshadowed by dominant discourses.

There are multiple markers of identity that constitute the subaltern, such as race, class, caste, ethnicity and religion. The term recognises individual identity as a plural concept and analyses it as fluid and heterogeneous. In *Selections from the Prison Notebooks* (1971), the Italian Marxist philosopher Antonio Gramsci (1891–1937) defined the subaltern classes as a section of the civil society who 'are not unified and cannot unite' unless they can become a 'State', implying that they cannot assert their existence unless they attain power (52). Their history, he observes, is woven within the fabric of the civil society and thus, bound together with the history of the state. However, the existence of these subaltern classes lies latent within the collective records which constitute the official history of the state.

The European subaltern was identified as the worker or the poor. Gramsci proposed a methodology to study these subaltern classes. This included a study of the process of the formation of subaltern groups on the basis of economic production – their origins, transformations, affiliations to dominant groups and assertions of autonomy. He observes that the dominant groups exert a continuous ideological influence on the subaltern groups through hegemonic practices, while the latter, in turn, attempt to remould these dominant ideologies by infusing into them their own claims. This continuous interaction and osmosis between the dominant and subaltern groups leads to a pattern of 'decomposition, renovation and neo-formation' (Gramsci 202). Consequently, the subaltern groups acquire an amorphous quality of existence which is porous and subject to continuous transformations. Gramsci arrives at the conclusion that mapping a history of the parties of the subaltern groups as a collective is a complex process. More so, because such a process would involve a detailed understanding of the repercussions of the actions of the parties on the subaltern groups collectively and on the attitudes of the dominant groups, as well as the impacts of the actions of the dominant groups on the subaltern groups.

Focusing on the marginalised and the dispossessed thus, Subaltern Studies as a theoretical approach is firmly rooted in a political – particularly, Marxist – ideology. Karl Marx classifies society into two opposing categories – the bourgeoisie and the proletariat. The bourgeoisie owns the means of production, while the proletariat is defined as the wage-earner. In his classification of the subaltern, Gramsci comes closer to the Marxist concept of the proletariat as he points out that the subaltern groups are subject to a certain dominant 'hegemony' – implying rule by consent – and that their history is 'necessarily fragmented and episodic', suggesting an intrinsic pattern of discontinuity or gaps in narration (55). The nature of this discontinuity in narration is also varied, and mainstream historiography documenting the progress of a society at large tends to further obliterate these gaps by imparting to the essentially fragmented narrative of diversity a seemingly uninterrupted flow of continuity.

However, while the Marxist concept of identifying the subaltern on the basis of their class position holds true for the European understanding of the subaltern, in the non-European and particularly Indian, context, the category constituting the subaltern is not confined to being subjugated in terms of class. A plurality of other factors such as race, caste, gender and ethnicity combine with the subjugation imposed by class, thereby problematising the idea of subalternity. This results in Subaltern Studies as a perspective acquiring a range of human and cultural references much larger than the specifications in Gramsci's original delineation, in terms of group as well as individual identity.

For instance, postcolonial studies locate in the voice of the colonised a subaltern perspective of history. This can be further discussed in the context of the work and ideas of Edward Said. Said in *Orientalism* (1978) explains the Eurocentric concept of the Orient as being culturally produced by the ideological justifications of the coloniser. He defines the Orient as essentially an idea in the Eurocentric mind and as endowed with a history and cultural presence validating its reality for the West, irrespective of its actual constitution or existence. These thoughts, largely rooted in the Eurocentric imagination, emphasise the *otherness* of the colonised. They exclude the voices and cultures of the natives who constitute, for the West, a domain of subjects justifiably ruled and dominated by those (colonisers) who 'know' them and 'know' what is good for them, better than they themselves do.

As Michel Foucault argues, since knowledge is sanctioned through power and power is constituted through accepted forms of knowledge, so the Western knowledge based on a Eurocentric understanding of the Orient 'grows among signs, from book to book, in the interstice of repetitions and commentaries' (*Orientalism* 91). These representations of the Orient, based on the Western imagination, 're-present' and consolidate the nature of difference constituted by the Orient in terms of a binary perception. The 'otherness' of the Orient is therefore constituted and enforced upon the Western imagination through a process of continuous repetitions; and this comes to be recognised as 'knowledge', and it is this knowledge – widely accepted and transmitted as sanctioned information about the Orient – that forms the legitimised foundation of comprehending the Orient and indigenous populations. Said was influenced by Gramsci and Fanon in his conceptualisation of the Orient as a cultural construct. In his *The Wretched of the Earth* (1961), from a psychoanalytical perspective, Frantz Fanon describes decolonisation as an essentially violent process. According to him, the dominant narratives and structures remain that of the coloniser, only to be inherited by the colonised intellectual. He observes that as soon as the coloniser begins an interaction with the native/colonised, they infiltrate the native culture with Western values and morality. To the coloniser, the native is the 'deforming element, disfiguring all that has to do with beauty or morality' (41). In the process, the coloniser dehumanises the native who is then evaluated and represented by the former so as to construct a cultural opposition to White supremacy and Christian benevolence. In the process, the colonised native is subalternised by being denied their own voice and being *spoken for* by the oppressor/coloniser.

Fanon further observes that during the period of decolonisation, the colonisers engage in 'a dialogue' with the 'colonized intellectuals', while 'the indigenous population is seen as a blurred mass' bereft of any individual identity (44). This group of colonised intellectuals who connect with the colonisers and attain an understanding of the latter's values and world order, go on to re-shape and adopt the same values for their own nation, once liberated from the colonial rule. Far from representing the masses or working to serve their interests, these colonised intellectuals negotiate their own elitist agendas under the influence of Western thoughts and ideals. Postcolonial histories therefore, tend to perpetuate the discourses generated by the bourgeoisie among the erstwhile coloniser, thereby marginalising the common people who constitute the subaltern.

An example of this phenomenon in the context of India may be seen in the formation of the Indian National Congress in 1885. Formed as a body to represent 'Indian' interests at the initiative of Allan Octavian Hume, the main motive behind the formation of the Congress was to provide a platform for civic and political dialogue between Indians and the British. However, the presidents and representatives of the Congress over the years largely belonged to the educated elite who were familiar with and influenced by English ideals and education. This so-called platform for 'Indian' representation, hence, had little to do with the faceless crowd of common people comprising peasants, working classes and indigenous populations. Though under the leadership of Mohandas Karamchand Gandhi, the Indian nationalist movement initiated by the Congress did acquire the form of a mass movement, the interests of the masses did not feature in the political agenda of the party. Meanwhile, several alternative nationalist movements based on different ideologies which were prevalent during this time were completely obliterated from the mainstream historiography documenting Indian nationalism.

In *The Wretched of the Earth*, Fanon goes beyond the concept of the Marxist proletariat in the general composition of an indigenous population, and refers to the 'lumpenproletariat' – the category defined by Marx as the poorest of the poor who hold no significance for the nation. According to Fanon, the lumpenproletariat, comprising non-industrial workers, peasantry and indigenous people, constitute a category of the colonised who are free from the hegemonic constructs of colonial cultural discourse. They, therefore, form a direct opposition to colonised intellectuals and elites. According to Fanon, it is this class which 'constitutes one of the most spontaneous and the most radically revolutionary forces of a colonized people', capable of revolting against the colonial status quo (129). They comprise the subaltern sections of the population, existing in tandem with the mainstream, whose histories and cultures remain largely undocumented. The many peasant uprisings and tribal insurgencies in India may be cited as familiar examples of nationalist struggles which involved several small communities and were carried out without any elitist support or leadership.

THE SUBALTERN STUDIES GROUP

In the South Asian and particularly Indian context, a group of scholars working on Subaltern Studies emerged in the 1980s. This Subaltern Studies group was founded by Ranajit Guha and was led by Indian scholars and historians like Guha, Gautam Bhadra, Sumit Sarkar, Tanika Sarkar, Partha Chatterjee, Dipesh

Chakrabarty and Gyanendra Pandey, and British scholars like David Arnold and David Hardiman. It aimed at exploring the latent presence and unrecorded assertions of subaltern sections of the population. Offering an alternative discourse to the elitist nationalist historiography, the Subaltern Studies group, known as the Subaltern Studies Collective, brought out annually, beginning from 1982, collections of essays titled *Subaltern Studies: Writings on South Asian History and Society*. Apart from identifying and defining the subaltern in the Indian context, these volumes offer detailed analyses of several peasant insurgencies. They attempt to delineate a deliberate pattern in mainstream history and nationalist politics that tends to obliterate subaltern movements that challenged colonial rule in India, and to dismiss them as inconsequential, sporadic, or as devoid of logic.

THEORISING SUBALTERN STUDIES

The European understanding of subaltern uprisings had largely identified this section of the population as 'pre-political' following the theoretical contributions of E. J. Hobsbawm. Hobsbawm defines the poor men and women comprising the rebels from the peasantry as 'pre-political' in *Primitive Rebels* (1959), and describes them as people who rose against authorities without apparently well-defined nationalist motives but voiced the general interest of the masses. In the chapter titled 'The Social Bandit', he argues that the term 'bandit' must concern the social historian conceptually, because 'banditry is a rather primitive form of organized social protest', and refers to the prototype represented in the figure of Robin Hood (13). However, Hobsbawm denies to this form of social protest any political character. Pointing out this Western perception of the subaltern, Ranajit Guha observes in his introduction to *Elementary Aspects of Peasant Insurgency in Colonial India* (1983), how traditional historiography treats the peasant–rebel as an individual with a historically verifiable existence but not someone who has consciously, through their logic and consent, been a part of any rebellion against the power hierarchy. The implication is that the subaltern existed as a 'simpleton' without any overt knowledge of principles, beliefs or structured organisation.

Guha negates this perspective. Referring to the history of subaltern uprisings in India in the context of land and agrarian reforms through the nineteenth and twentieth centuries, he observes that in order to do justice to the peasant–rebel, one must accept them as conscious individuals with their own understanding of their own world, and acknowledge their impetus to change the existing world order. This realisation confers upon the subaltern an individuality, and understanding of the political as distinctly separate from the mainstream perception. Guha refutes the general tendency of official historiography to record peasant insurgencies like the one led by Titumir in Bengal in 1831, as 'purely spontaneous' episodes in the colonial history of India (4). He observes that such an idea which denies political thought and existence to the subaltern is 'elitist as well as erroneous' (4), and refers to Gramsci's observation that no historical event is purely spontaneous and argues that these apparently unstructured events organised by the masses have their own political validity. Guha critiques Hobsbawm's view of 'pre-political' people and populations based on an apparent absence of explicit ideologies or organisation, and asserts that in the militant uprisings organised by the rural people in colonial India against semi-feudal structures of ruthless exploitation, there was nothing which was not political.

In his preface to *Subaltern Studies, Volume I*, Guha defines 'subaltern' as a term signifying subordination or subjugation in the South Asian society. This subjugation can be constituted in terms of caste, gender, age, class, social position or any other component of identity. He discards the subject-position adopted by mainstream nationalist historiographers such as Surendra Nath Sen as it constitutes an exclusive historical record of the Indian elite where the political consciousness and assertions of identity by the subaltern population go unrecorded. He declares that the aim of the Subaltern Studies group would be to function as 'a measure of objective assessment of the role of the elite' as well as 'a critique of elitist interpretations of that role' (vii). In this manner, Subaltern Studies seeks to re-inscribe a subject-position to the subaltern by scrutinising minutely the approach of elitist documentation towards subaltern narratives in history.

Guha observes that the history of India comprises two parallel narratives – one officially recorded and archived and the other an independent autonomous domain which constitutes the 'politics of the people' (Guha, *SS I* 4). The latter is subsumed by the sweeping generalisations made by the former. In this process, an invisible power hierarchy becomes functional in the presentation of history as a coherent, linear and structured narrative. He refers to the anti-Rowlatt upsurge of 1919 and the Quit India movement of 1942 as examples of mass movements which defied all attempts at elitist control. Guha concludes that the prime shortcoming of mainstream historiography is its failure to accept or comprehend the original efforts and contribution of the common people, independent of the elite, towards the development of nationalism. For instance, even the anti-Rowlatt upsurge and Quit India movement are highlighted as Gandhian movements in the representation of history – the first as ushering in the Gandhian era in Indian politics, while the second as launched under the leadership of Gandhi with the famous slogan, 'do or die'. However, what helped these movements have an impact on the British rule is not the presence of a specific leader–representative or a particular ideology, but the large-scale participation of the common masses who formed the 'faceless' crowd compelling the colonisers to acknowledge resistance.

Nonetheless, elitist historiography does not give any importance to this faceless crowd whose individual identities are enshrouded by a homogenised narrative of predetermined ideology and political ends. Bestowing individual subject-positions upon these people or tracing their subjective narratives constitutes the process of unravelling the subaltern. Identifying the category of the subaltern, as opposed to the elite, in fact, poses a major challenge to scholars and researchers. This arises from the possibility of an individual belonging to either of these groups under different contexts and situations. The semi-feudal structure of colonial India accounted for a porous social fabric. At the regional and local levels, the category constituting the elite, for instance, was heterogeneous. Depending upon the class being referred to, certain groups such as the poor rural gentry, impoverished landlords, rich peasants and upper-middle-class peasants who normally ranked among the elite in the local scenario, could under certain circumstances and situations comprise the subaltern. This made it difficult to compartmentalise people clearly as either elite or subaltern. The situation is not very different in the post-Independence context either. The social fabric is still porous and an individual who holds an elite position in the rural context, for instance, might still belong to the subaltern section when placed in the urban scenario.

Focusing on the instances of the innumerable peasant insurgencies in colonial India, *Subaltern Studies I* explores the socio-historical reality of the subaltern with reference to the existing agrarian equations. While David Arnold explores the Gudem Rampa Rebellion of 1839–1924, Gyanendra Pandey provides a detailed analysis of the peasant movement in Awadh, 1919–22. Arnold refers to the violent peasant uprisings in the hill tracts of Gudem and Rampa in Andhra Pradesh, and noting how these insurgencies have been overlooked by mainstream historiographical records, observes that, 'peasants appear as the victims of history, not as its principals' (Guha, *SS I* 89). Pandey's article, titled 'Peasant Revolt and Indian Nationalism, 1919–1922', offers an account of the peasant uprisings in Awadh against the British system of exploitation, which occurred around 1921. These uprisings were led by local leaders voicing their protest against the local *taluqdars* and landowners who were their immediate oppressors. Pandey notes that 'nationalist as well as colonialist commentators tended to treat the "masses" as essentially inert' (Guha, *SS I* 151). He traces the political developments which led to mainstream elitist interventions and a subsequent suppression of what began as a people's movement under the Awadh Kisan Sabha.

David Hardiman, in 'The Indian "Faction": A Political Theory Examined', makes a close study of the historical events which led to the formation of such factions. His research in based on the history of the Indian nationalist movement in the district of Kheda in Gujarat. He studies the role played by the community known as 'Patidars' in the nationalist movement in the district under the leadership of people like Sardar Vallabhbhai Patel and Darbar

Gopaldas. Hardiman argues that both Patel and Gopaldas declared themselves as Gandhian nationalists 'to undermine the power' of their 'old rivals, the Nadiad Desais', who formed the opposing faction of the powerful Patidars (Guha, *SS I* 204). Hence, the rise of Gandhian nationalism in Kheda serves as 'a clear case of factionalism' (204). He concludes that these factions that were formed at various points in history by the coming together of two or more subaltern classes under a given situation, were random and unstable, and more often than not, they had no ideological parameters attached to them. They were forged by immediate interests, and loyalties were determined accordingly. This tendency towards factionalism makes it even more difficult to ascribe a clear subjective-position to the subaltern because the criteria determining subalternity are amorphous, diffused and overlapping.

Hence, the identity of the subaltern is enshrouded in an invisible margin of historical non-existence along with inadequate documentation and overlapping markers inscribing individuality in terms of categories such as class, caste, community, ethnicity and race. Guha in *Subaltern Studies II* observes that even when documented, the gaze to which the subaltern is subjected by historians may largely be classified into three categories. He refers to these categories as constituting the primary, secondary and tertiary ranges of discourse, based upon documentation. The primary sources of documentation are mostly official and their chief characteristic is their immediacy. The secondary sources draw on the primary sources and transform them at the same time. They are later documentations intended to be read by the people. The tertiary discourse is defined by Guha as that which is distant and remote from the event it represents and looks upon the event from the objective distance of omniscience. These categories of documentation comprise the multiple gazes that the subaltern is subjected to in the process of identification and research.

The voice of the subaltern, as also their identity, undergoes a series of representations before being eventually documented in mainstream history. An important example in this case is offered by Jhalkaribai (1830–58), the attendant and fellow warrior of Rani Lakshmibai in the uprising of 1857. While various historians and novelists have provided descriptions of the siege of Jhansi in 1857 and the heroic resistance of Lakshmibai, few have mentioned the subaltern Jhalkaribai belonging to the kori caste or elaborated upon her contribution. She closely resembled Lakshmibai in terms of her appearance, and sacrificed her life camouflaged as the Rani of Jhansi when the English conquered the fort, thereby providing Lakshmibai with the time and opportunity to escape the massacre. Jhalkaribai drew the attention of writers and historians in the late twentieth century. Her subalternity was constituted by her caste as well as class positions. In 2001, a commemorative postage stamp on Jhalkaribai was issued by the Department of Post, India, recognising her role in the First War of Indian Independence. In his book titled *Women Heroes and Dalit Assertion in North India: Culture, Identity and Politics* (2006), Badri Narayan observes how 'today, the Koris, like other Dalit castes, use the myth of Jhalkaribai for the glorification of their community' and adds that 'they also celebrate *Jhalkaribai Jayanti* each year to enhance their self-respect and elevate the status of their caste' (119).

The fact that subalternity, in a given context, space or time, is not constituted as a compartmentalised domain but has overlapping factors which lend it an amorphous nature, may be seen in how in the same context of the 1857 Uprising, even Lakshmibai has been read and represented as a subaltern by various writers and historians on the basis of gender. One of the earliest portrayals of Lakshmibai may be found in the novel *Seeta* (1872) by Philip Meadows Taylor. The Rani has continued to be represented through the late-twentieth and twenty-first centuries in works such as *Nightrunners of Bengal* (1951) by John Masters, *Jhansir Rani* (1956) by Mahasweta Devi, and *Rani* (2007) by Jaishree Misra. The figure of Lakshmibai has continued to baffle creative and historical imagination by representing a nonconformist woman who actively took part in the battle to defend her own kingdom. This domain of active participation in a battle has always been understood as a masculinist domain, according to patriarchal standards. Lakshmibai is, therefore, perceived as a symbol of transgression of gender codes and her life, consequently, has been an area of creative inquiry for writers from different nationalities across the centuries.

> **SUBALTERN STUDIES IN LATIN AMERICA**
>
> A major extension of the Indian Subaltern Studies Collective evolved in Latin America in the 1990s. The cause of the subaltern and the necessity to explore these marginalised voices had gained prominence in the 1970s. On the model of Subaltern Studies as an academic approach framed by the Indian Collective, the Latin American Subaltern Studies group was founded by John Beverley (a literary and cultural critic based at the University of Pittsburgh, who specialised on Spanish and Latin American Literature), Ileana Rodríguez (Nicaragua), Robert Carr (Trinidad), José Rabasa and Javier Sanjinés (Bolivia), in 1993. The purpose of the group was to critique 'the limits of elite historiography in relation to the subaltern', as stated in the article titled 'Founding Statement' in *The Postmodernism Debate in Latin America* (1995). The group further explains that three social movements defined the outlines and concerns of Latin American Subaltern Studies – the Mexican, Cuban and Nicaraguan revolutions. The idea of identifying the subaltern in Latin America arises from the need to redefine the manner in which the concepts of 'nation', 'state' and 'people' came to be related or associated with each other through these three social movements. The topic of subalternity in the Latin American context, therefore, is addressed in three major phases.

THE PRAXIS OF SUBALTERN HISTORIOGRAPHY

Analysing the role of time–space axes in the determination of subalternity across the South Asian and Latin American contexts, Rodríguez observes that the theoretical basis of identifying the subaltern is a presumption of superiority. This, in turn, results in the formation of two distinct streams of epistemology – one identified as elite, and the other as subaltern. The process of subordination and the mechanisms of hegemony can be understood only from the subject-position of the subaltern. It is this requirement of locating the subaltern and understanding hegemony and subordination from their perspective, that releases Subaltern Studies as a theoretical approach from the domains of a single academic discipline. Since dominance and subjugation may be articulated through diverse social and cultural practices, their manifestations in the undocumented records might occur in several forms of oral or written representations. Each form of utterance is studied within its own theoretical praxis. However, these domains merge and overlap in the case of Subaltern Studies.

In *Philosophy of History*, M. C. Lemon mentions two kinds of approaches adopted by scholars of history – speculative and analytic. The speculative philosophy of history, he observes, stems from a desire to make sense of history or discern an intelligible pattern in it. It is, in a way, a futuristic attempt to make sense of history. The introduction of a counter-hegemonic discourse from the position of the subaltern into the domains of existing mainstream historiographical narratives makes an attempt to rediscover lost identities in the larger all-encompassing homogenised and seemingly coherent narrative of a nation. It, therefore, needs, to an extent, the speculative angle of history in order to trace the existence of the subaltern in a sweepingly grand nationalist narrative. Being largely undocumented and unarchived, the subaltern require means of representations transcending the boundaries of accepted archives sanctified as 'history', in order to rediscover and re-assert their presence lost in the interstices of dominant history.

Such archives interrogate the monologic parameters and claims for singularity by an academic discipline. They comprise cultural manifestations – latent or prominent, embedded in the social framework. In his introduction to *Culture and Imperialism* (1993), Said writes of culture as 'a source of identity', and observes that interpreting it in terms of the hybridity of historical experiences, defines it as 'a sort of theatre where various political and ideological causes engage one another' (xiv). He observes that each culture attempts to define itself in terms of its distinctiveness from the other. This distinctiveness is made apparent by its own intrinsic features such as language, occasions, national feasts, basic texts and so on, which make it stand out as different from other cultures. The socio-cultural implication of the term 'subaltern', thus, comes to associate itself with a variety of forms asserting identity – ranging from personal documents, oral traditions, indigenous occasions and festivities, to the more accepted aesthetic forms of representation such as arts, films and literature. Traditional elitist historiography overlooks these domains as sites of resistance of the subaltern population.

Ranajit Guha acknowledges this inadequacy of mainstream historiography and writes that such historical narratives clearly exclude the politics and political assertions of the people. It denies them their existence as subjects within a particular context of the nation and society. Legitimising the importance of alternative modes of documentation in the context of peasant rebellions, Partha Chatterjee argues, in 'Agrarian Relations and Communalism in Bengal, 1926–1935', that within the power hierarchy of a feudal society at any point of time, there cannot be possibly any direct exchange of correspondence between a feudal landlord and his community. However, in each specific case under scrutiny one may discern visible symbols of feudal authority in the rituals and customs which represent feudal right and property. These forms of expression embedded within the culture of the community thereby provide a documentation of certain events and their impact from the subaltern perspective.

It is in this manner that the voices of the subaltern and their patterns of existence are assimilated as an invisible presence within layers of social life. The researcher of Subaltern Studies must consider these fragmented, unofficial, de-chronologised, suggestive and obscure narratives, in order to reconstruct the subject-position of the subaltern. As a result, subaltern historiography connects with cultural anthropology, interrogating and analyzing the non-verbal narratives of latent voices. In *Reading Subaltern Studies* (2002), David Ludden notes that there can be no singular stream of studying or documenting the intellectual history of subalternity, because its articulations are embedded in spatio-temporal diversity and manifested as dissimilar from each other. Each subaltern utterance is, thus, distinct in itself.

★★★

While the Subaltern Studies Collective focused on the existence and contribution of the subaltern in the framing of nationalist historiography through documentation and analysis of various peasant insurgencies, the socio-cultural implication of the term 'subaltern' is too vast to be contained in a singularised domain of academic discourse. The subaltern does not constitute an insulated domain of homogeneous identity. Within the same group identified as subaltern, there are differences which divide the perspective and subject-position of one individual or community from the other. To use the term 'subaltern' as a blanket term to imply the voiceless and underprivileged would lead to what Amartya Sen calls 'miniaturization of human beings' in *Identity and Violence* (185). As seen in the case of Jhalkaribai and Rani Lakshmibai, even individuals belonging to two completely different classes or caste positions might comprise subalternity within the same historical context, depending upon a different marker of identity – in this case, gender.

Towards the end of the twentieth century, with the changing concepts and understanding of the terms 'nation' and 'identity', and the gradual rise of a transnational global diaspora, the connotations of the term 'subaltern' have also undergone changes. On the one hand, there has been a huge increase in immigration from one continent to another. On the other hand, there also have been more instances of blatant assertion of power through fundamentalist and majoritarian claims. This, in turn, has led to the fragmentation of the world even beyond the Three Worlds theory. The emergence of multiple worlds and the hybridity of a plethora of communities through immigration and intermarriage, has resulted in the expansion of the term 'subaltern' to include the innumerable marginalised voices and minorities across various geographical areas.

REFERENCES

Amin, Shahid, and Dipesh Chakrabarty, ed. *Subaltern Studies IX: Writings on South Asian History and Society*. Oxford UP, 1996.

Arnold, David, and David Hardiman, ed. *Subaltern Studies VIII: Essays in Honour of Ranajit Guha*. Oxford UP, 1994.

Bhadra, Gautam, Gyan Prakash, and Susie Tharu, ed. *Subaltern Studies X: Writings on South Asian History and Society*. Oxford UP, 1999.

Beverley, John. *Testimonio: On the Politics of Truth*. U of Minnesota P, 2004.

Beverley, John, et al, ed. *The Postmodernism Debate in Latin America.* Duke UP, 1995.

Chatterjee, Partha. 'Agrarian Relations and Communalism in Bengal, 1926–1935'. *Subaltern Studies I: Writings on South Asian History and Society.* Ed. Ranajit Guha. Oxford UP, 1982. 9–38.

Chatterjee, Partha, and Gyanendra Pandey, ed. *Subaltern Studies VII: Writings on South Asian History and Society.* Oxford UP, 1992.

Chatterjee, Partha, and Pradeep Jeganathan, ed. *Subaltern Studies XI: Community, Gender and Violence.* Orient Blackswan, 2002.

Choudhuri, Indranath. 'Traditions of Folk in Literature'. <http://www.indranathchoudhuri.com/Articles%20new%20new/3/Traditions%20of%20folk%20in%20Literature.pdf>.

----, ed. *Encyclopaedia of Indian Literature, Volume II.* Sahitya Akademi, 2009.

Fanon, Frantz. *The Wretched of the Earth.* 1961. Penguin, 1967.

Foucault, Michel. *Language, Counter-Memory, Practice. Select Essays and Interviews.* Ed. Donald F Bouchard. Cornell UP, 1980.

Gramsci, Antonio. *Selections from the Prison Notebooks.* International Publishers, 1971.

Guha, Ranajit. *Elementary Aspects of Peasant Insurgency in Colonial India.* Oxford UP, 1983.

----, ed. *Subaltern Studies I: Writings on South Asian History and Society.* Oxford UP, 1982.

----, ed. *Subaltern Studies II: Writings on South Asian History and Society.* Oxford UP, 1983.

----, ed. *Subaltern Studies III: Writings on South Asian History and Society.* Oxford UP, 1984.

----, ed. *Subaltern Studies IV: Writings on South Asian History and Society.* Oxford UP, 1985.

----, ed. *Subaltern Studies V: Writings on South Asian History and Society.* Oxford UP, 1987.

----, ed. *Subaltern Studies VI: Writings on South Asian History and Society.* Oxford UP, 1989.

Hobsbawm, E. J. *Primitive Rebels.* Abacus, 2017.

Lemon, M.C. *Philosophy of History.* Routledge, 2003.

Ludden, David ed. *Reading Subaltern Studies.* Permanent Black, 2002.

Marx, Karl, and Friedrich Engels. *The Communist Manifesto*. Lerner Publishing Group, Inc., 2018. <https://www.bard.edu/library/arendt/pdfs/Marx-CommunistManifesto.pdf>

Manuel, George, and Michael Poslun. *The Fourth World: An Indian Reality*. 1974. U of Minnesota P, 2019.

Narayan, Badri. *Women Heroes and Dalit Assertion in North India: Culture, Identity and Politics*. Sage, 2006.

Rodriguez, Ileana, ed. *The Latin American Subaltern Studies Reader*. Duke UP, 2001.

Said, Edward. *Orientalism*. Pantheon, 1978.

----. *Culture and Imperialism*. Vintage, 1994.

Savarkar, V. D. *The Indian War of Independence 1857*. Rajdhani Granthagar, 1970.

Sen, Amartya. *Identity and Violence*. Penguin, 2006.

Sen, Surendra Nath. *Eighteen Fifty-Seven*. Publications Division, 1957.

Singh, Amritjit, and Peter Schmidt. *Postcolonial Theory and the United States: Race, Ethnicity and Literature*. UP of Mississippi, 2000.

Spivak, Gayatri Chakravarty. 'Can the Subaltern Speak?'. *Literary Theory: An Introductory Reader*. Ed. Saugata Bhaduri and Simi Malhotra. Anthem Press, 2010. 263–318.

----. *In Other Worlds*. Routledge, 1988.

Chapter Two

The Subaltern Studies Collective

The Subaltern Studies Collective was founded by Ranajit Guha in India in the 1980s. In the preface to the first volume of *Subaltern Studies: Writings on South Asian History and Society*, Guha states that the aim of the group is to 'promote a systematic and informed discussion of the subaltern themes in the field of South Asian studies' so as to 'rectify the elitist bias' in most of the research and academic work in this area (*SS I* vii). With contributions from scholars across the world such as Partha Chatterjee, Shahid Amin, David Arnold, Gyanendra Pandey, David Hardiman, Gautam Bhadra, Dipesh Chakrabarty, Sumit Sarkar, Tanika Sarkar, Susie Tharu and Swapan Dasgupta, the collections of essays brought out by the group investigated various nuances of subalternity through explorations of relatively obscure chapters from the collective history of India as a nation.

The academic response to the work of the Subaltern Studies Collective was varied. The conventional scholars found it difficult to acknowledge the gaps in historical archives, which were identified by the group. The very concept of Subaltern Studies ushered in global collaborations and dialogue among academic researchers, raising questions about the lost subaltern utterances, which could not be answered by conventional historiography. As a result, the project expanded in its scope, and in the preface to the fourth volume, Guha noted that although originally planned as a series of three volumes, the collection would continue its journey, and a new section for discussions was included in the volume to accommodate global dialogue and interventions. The *Subaltern Studies* collection finally took the form of twelve volumes published between 1982 and 2005, of which the first six volumes were edited by Guha. The rest were edited by other scholars associated with the project.

THE THEORETICAL UNDERPINNINGS

Though based on the Marxist ideas of class division and subjugation, and inspired by Gramsci's conceptualisation of the subaltern in *Selections from the Prison Notebooks of Antonio Gramsci* (1971), the Subaltern Studies group began its journey through a meticulous reworking and appropriation of these concepts to apply them to the Indian context. As discussed in the previous chapter, the concept of the subaltern defined by Gramsci in the Italian context or based on the Western experience, was significantly different from its manifestations in India. In post-Independence India, the structure of the state had evolved from the earlier feudal order to resemble the Eurocentric nation state, through the transfer of power in 1947. The political parties in the newly formed democracy strove to consolidate their power over the nation state, while the dominant elite continued to rule the public domain of knowledge. In the process, the subaltern population who had been active participants in the resistance against foreign rule was further marginalised, almost to the point of invisibility. In his article titled 'Gramsci in India: Homage to a Teacher' (2007), Ranajit Guha observes that in order to understand the role of the state in the Indian context, the Subaltern Studies group 'relied on the Hegelian master–servant dialectic and the Gramscian theory of hegemony' (*The Small Voice of History* 365). The Hegelian master–slave relationship was one of pure domination and enabled an understanding of the elite and the subaltern as two independent self-consciousnesses encountering one another and engaging in a struggle. The Gramscian concept of cultural hegemony was more complex in gesturing towards socially structured norms that insidiously legitimised this domination by inducing the servant to accept and interiorise their inferiority. This model served to explain the sociological stratification and the consequent process of subjugation.

In 'Gramsci in India', Guha also notes that despite there being two mainstream communist parties in the Indian political front, the Subaltern Studies group maintained its distance from them, because ideologically these political parties 'represented a left-liberal extension of the Indian power elite itself' (*The Small Voice of History* 362). The emergence of the group was sparked off by the Naxal movement (1968–71) – a militant peasant movement in North Bengal which drew its inspiration from the Chinese revolution and ideas of Mao Zedong. Raging across the Naxalbari area of the northern part of West Bengal, and directed against the oppression of the landless peasantry and itinerant farm workers at the hands of landlords, moneylenders, police and upper-caste aristocrats, the Naxalbari movement engendered a peculiar alliance of the peasant and the intellectual. Inspired by leftist ideology, young intellectuals from urban areas – mostly students – abandoned their careers to join this movement of resistance against exploitation. This, in turn, led to the destabilisation of the standardised social hierarchies in rural areas that had justified exploitation of the weak on grounds of the hegemonic law of natural inheritance. The movement strengthened over time and led to several instances of rebellion in different parts of rural Bengal where oppressive landlords were murdered by Naxalite groups.

Guha states that the Subaltern Studies group 'started working together in the mid-1970s when the Naxalite upsurge had clearly subsided, although the questions it had provoked were still unanswered' (*The Small Voice of History* 364). An inquiry into the colonial history of India only highlighted these concerns further because the assertion of power in colonial India was not only between the coloniser and the colonised. At different levels of complexities within the social fabric, power dynamics could be seen to be actively operative between the dominant and the dominated in the civil society in terms of caste, class, gender, religion and other indigenous hierarchies. According to Guha, the historical articulation of power in all its aspects can be understood as 'an interaction of Dominance and Subordination', and he further suggests that hegemony presents a condition where 'Dominance enables Persuasion to outweigh Coercion' (366). Within this definition, Guha situates the popular mass movements during the Indian struggle for independence and also the domain of Gandhian politics which acquired popular consent through the support it received from the elites, thereby becoming acceptable to the lower classes. Guha notes that the development of the Indian nation through the decades after Independence led to a further steepening of this inherent traditional divide and a growing discontent amongst the dominated. This resulted in a 'twofold generational discontent', where the older generation was disillusioned by the failed promises of a happier future, while the younger generation was disillusioned by the bleak future that awaited them (*The Small Voice of History* 364). It was this twofold generational discontent which characterised the Naxalite movement and also served as the impetus for the Subaltern Studies group (where Guha represented the older generation, while the others were much younger than him). Guha highlights this ontological detail of the group 'to indicate that our project was an organic part of its life and times' and 'not just a detached academic observation' (364). Accordingly, the collections of essays published by the Subaltern Studies group provide an overall study of the Indian society through an investigation of the gaps in mainstream history which obliterated subaltern voices.

A CRITICAL SURVEY OF IMPORTANT CONTRIBUTIONS

In the preface to the second volume, Ranajit Guha states that the main objective of Subaltern Studies would be the 'acknowledgement of the subaltern as the maker of his own history and the architect of his own destiny' (*SS II* vii). As discussed in the first chapter, this endowing of the subaltern with a political consciousness is what distinguishes the approach of Subaltern Studies from Hobsbawm's classification of the peasantry as 'pre-political'. In his article titled 'The Prose of Counter-Insurgency' (1983), Guha notes that the multiplicity of conditions which constituted the subalternity of the peasant were 'materialized by the structure of property, institutionalized by law' and 'sanctified by religion', so much so that the subaltern 'had too much at stake' and would not launch into rebellion except as a 'deliberate, even if, desperate way out of the intolerable condition of existence' (*SS II* 2). Hence, the articulations of subaltern resistance in history cannot be overlooked as spontaneous or reflex actions on the part of the peasants without a defined political consciousness. However, since the primary archival sources often carry the legacy of elitist perspectives, as they are recorded by the dominant groups, the subaltern voice is lost through the gaps in the narrative structure.

Gautam Bhadra, another founder member of the group, revisits the historical archives of Mughal India in his essay 'Two Uprisings in Mughal India' (1983). Tracing the rebellion of Sanatan Sardar in the seventeenth century during Emperor Jahangir's reign, and the consequent Hatikheda Rebellion in 1621 along the area of Cooch Bihar and the borders of Assam, Bhadra states that the history of India is replete with instances of numerous subaltern uprisings against the dominant powers. However, these narratives – lost to mainstream historiography – await rediscovery by scholars and historians. He argues that the role played by these rebellions is of such pivotal political importance that they compel historians to 'revalue a hitherto submerged and neglected tradition' (*SS II* 43).

In a later essay titled 'Four Rebels of Eighteen-Fifty-Seven' (1985) published in the fourth volume of *Subaltern Studies*, Bhadra writes that in the entire range of documenting nationalist history 'what has been missed out is the ordinary rebel, *his* role and *his* perception of alien rule and contemporary crisis' (*SS IV* 230). Bhadra enumerates the roles played by four rebels during the 1857 uprising, who are now completely lost to history: Shah Mal (a small landlord of Bijraul), Devi Singh (a rebel belonging to a peasant community of Mathura), Gonoo (a kol leader from Singhbhum, Chotanagpore) and Ahmadullah Shah (a maulvi from Lucknow). He argues that these rebels cannot be read as faceless participants in an omnibus category called 'the people'. Similarly, they cannot be subsumed as components in a linear tradition which would lead to the appropriation of power by the elite in the post-colonial state. Bhadra calls for a 'new historiography' which would 'seek after and restore the specific subjectivity of the rebels' (275).

The Subaltern Studies Collective, in their notion of the subaltern, included industrial workers as well as peasants. Dipesh Chakrabarty provides a detailed study of the working conditions of jute mill workers of Bengal, in his essay 'Conditions for Knowledge of Working-Class Conditions: Employers, Government and the Jute Workers of Calcutta, 1890–1940', published in the second volume of *Subaltern Studies* (1983). He examines various documents of the Indian Jute Mills Association, reports of the Indian Factory Labour Commission and letters exchanged between important officials, to detect the gaps and silences in the apparently structured narrative about the lives of the workers. Chakrabarty observes that 'the ruling-class documents often used for historical reconstructions of working-class conditions can be read both for what they say and for their "silences"' (*SS II* 259). In the deconstruction of these silences and gaps in narration, the historian must delve into an investigation of the working-class culture, moving away from purely economic explanations.

Chakrabarty shows that the culture of the jute mill workers in Calcutta (Kolkata) was very different from that of the workers assumed in Marx's works. The former was marked by primordial bonds of community, language, religion, caste and kinship. Hence, there was an inherent cultural gap between the priorities and outlook of the English employers and the native employees. While the former stressed upon keeping the factory machinery at work without breaks, to the latter these machines were almost magical and godly in their function. The workers' attitude towards the machines was defined by a religious fervour, not by scientific rationale. Therefore, in order to reconstruct a fairly accurate picture of the condition of the jute mill workers of Calcutta, the historian must be familiar with these nuances of culture because, Chakrabarty argues, 'in so far as that knowledge has a history, the gaps have a history too' *(SS II* 310).

Just as the diverse history of India is full of several episodes voicing the protests of the dominated and the subjugated, a careful scrutiny of twentieth-century nationalist movements also reflects multiple voices of subaltern dissent which were later homogenised to make them a part of a collective anti-imperial nationalist historical narrative. Shahid Amin puts forth a case study of such homogenisation in his essay titled 'Gandhi as Mahatma: Gorakhpur District, Eastern UP,

1921-22', published in the third volume of *Subaltern Studies* (1984). Providing a detailed analysis of the events which eventually led to the Chauri Chaura incident in February 1922, Amin shows how the popularity of the Gandhian Non-Cooperation Movement amongst the masses was not defined exactly by the projected Gandhian ideals of non-violence. The local population had their own experience of exploitation at the hands of foreign rulers and devised their own strategies to combat it, which was made to fit the functional political domain of the mainstream Gandhian movement. Amin writes, 'a "jaikar" [i.e., cheer] of adoration and adulation had become the rallying cry for direct action' (*SS III* 54). However, though the actions sought to justify themselves with reference to Gandhi, 'the Gandhi of its rustic protagonists was not as he really was, but as they had thought him up' (54). Such a political re-appropriation of Gandhi was made possible by the fact that there was no single version of Gandhi which the local peasants of eastern UP could have subscribed to. The Gandhi they followed was an imagined individual who reached them through oral versions constructed by the local leadership and whom they conjured up in their minds as the seat of order and authority. Amin further states that their ideas often 'clashed with the basic tenets of Gandhism itself', and therefore concludes that 'the violence of Chauri Chaura was rooted in this paradox' (55).

Partha Chatterjee further explores this enigma of Gandhism which dominates the anticolonial narrative of India's struggle for independence in his essay 'Gandhi and the Critique of Civil Society' (1984). He begins by citing Gandhi's own words from 'Discussion with Dharmadev' where Gandhi acknowledges that his 'language is aphoristic, it lacks precision. It is therefore open to several interpretations' (*SS III* 153). Chatterjee argues that unlike the other political theorists or activists of the early twentieth century, Gandhi's concept of nationalism rests on 'a fundamental critique of the idea of civil society'; for Gandhi, the reason for India's position as a colonised nation is the moral failure on the part of the Indians (156). According to him, India became a subject nation because it was enticed by the splendour of 'modern' Western civilisation. This was, in turn, based on the economic system of social production defined by a continuously expanding premise of production and demand. India had, therefore, been subordinated and colonised as a result of its moral failings and for being allured by the West. That is the reason why Gandhi's vision of nationalism rested on upholding khadi as the only sound economic proposition for a largely agrarian country like India, instead of heavy industrialisation which is imitating the West.

Similarly, Gandhi critiques secularisation of education because, according to him, this diminishes the ethical aspects of education and results in moral anarchy and licentious self-seeking through an exaggeration of social inequalities. Gandhi's utopian vision of a *Ramarajya*, Chatterjee explains, is 'a patriarchy, in which the ruler, by his moral quality and habitual adherence to truth, always expresses the collective will' (*SS III* 165). According to Chatterjee, it is this moral vision of an ideological utopia combined with the 'ideological baggage of nationalist politics' which enables Gandhism to open up 'the historical possibility by which the largest popular element of the nation, namely the peasantry, could be appropriated within the evolving political forms of the new Indian state' (193). In other words, Gandhian political vision empowered the elitist nationalist politics in India to assume the likeness of an authentic national movement through political mobilisation of the peasantry under the banner of non-violence. In the process, a national framework of politics is created where the 'peasants are mobilized but do not participate'; instead, they come to represent 'a nation of which they are a part but a nation state from which they are forever distanced' (194).

In the third volume, Sumit Sarkar, in 'The Conditions and Nature of Subaltern Militancy', observes that 'subaltern participation in anti-imperialist struggle is a sub-set within the broader theme of subaltern awakening' which is constituted through 'a variety of complex mediations' including 'the specific socio-economic structure of a region, historical traditions, efforts at mobilization by the elite – nationalist groups and ideologies – and British strategies' (*SS III* 276). Focusing on the socio-economic conditions of Bengal and engaging in a comparative study of the Swadeshi and Non-Cooperation movements, Sarkar highlights the contradictions evident in the historical picture of the age and analyses the reasons behind this display of divided sympathies in terms of class, caste and religion. He observes that the popularity of Gandhi was largely triggered by the magico-religious quality of the rumours centred around him. For instance, by February 1922, the Santals of Madarihat in Jalpaiguri had acquired a belief that they were immune to bullets as long as they were wearing Gandhi caps, and most popular mass movements were undertaken in his name. This led to the formation of a sort of cult – with the masses inhabiting the gaps between designed popular narratives, interspersed with half-informed initiatives. According to Sarkar, Gandhi evoked 'the mood of renunciation, austerity and sacrifice' – tenets which are 'deeply ingrained in the Hindu tradition' (314). He concludes that Gandhism presented a 'combination of peasant-populist religious idiom with strong urban bourgeois links and hard-headed organizational discipline mastering and channelizing autonomous outbursts' (320). Sarkar proposes a more systematic analysis of Gandhian nationalism to comprehend the variations within the homogenised structures of mainstream historiography.

Swapan Dasgupta's essay titled 'Adivasi Politics in Midnapur', published in the fourth volume of *Subaltern Studies*, provides a very different understanding of mainstream projections of political consciousness. Dasgupta focuses on the indigenous people of Midnapur, and particularly of the Jungle Mahals, which were inhabited by adivasi populations like the Santals, Bhumij and Kurmi, besides a substantial number of low-caste Hindus, such as the Bagdi, Goala and Sadgope. Providing an analysis of encroachment by statist powers and hierarchies, Dasgupta observes that 'economic change in the Jungle Mahals is an euphemism for the loss of political power of the adivasis' as alien structures of urban power are grafted on indigenous societies (*SS IV* 115). He elucidates how these acts of impingement by new communities of landowners and zamindars, resulting in the loss of land and economic deprivation, was considered by the adivasis as 'an affront to their dignity, their *izzat*, a theme recurrent in subaltern perception' and led to forms of violent uprisings (117). Citing examples from the extremist demonstrations of resistance displayed by the indigenous groups and manifested through diverse localised symbols of honour by use of indigenous weapons, Dasgupta asserts that 'what comes across from these acts of apparent fearlessness and solidarity is an alternative conception of justice born out of fundamentally different sets of values' (134). He rests his case on the fact that the rebels who were construed as criminals by the civil society did not comprehend their actions as criminal in nature, but rather believed in the justness of their struggle against invasive expansion of foreign rule.

Gayatri Chakravorty Spivak brings in the question of the woman as the gendered subaltern in her essay 'Subaltern Studies: Deconstructing Historiography' (1985). She critiques the group for overlooking the importance of the subaltern woman – who is doubly subjugated – as the concept-metaphor in the functionality of their discourse, and insists that 'a feminist historian of the subaltern must raise the question of woman as a structural rather than marginal issue' (*SS IV* 361). Spivak observes that throughout the historical instances of functional power hierarchies oppressing the powerless, the woman is objectified as she moves from clan to clan and family to family performing her gender role and is, in the process, drained of her individual identity. In the fifth volume of *Subaltern Studies*, Spivak exemplifies her point with reference to her translation of Mahasweta Devi's story *Stanadayini*. Discussed at length in the fourth chapter of the present book, the story is based on the life of a subaltern woman named Jashoda who works as a wet-nurse for her livelihood. Spivak uses the narrative to assert that literature complements historical archives by suggesting the plausibility of a Jashoda who could have existed as a subaltern in a specific historical moment and tested by orthodox assumptions. Her life, however, would not feature in the mainstream documentation of history, and the subaltern historian must unravel the text to assign a new subject-position to her in order to accommodate her voice as part of comprehending subalternity.

Adding the dimension of religion as a marker of identity imperative to the understanding of subalternity, Gyanendra Pandey provides a detailed analysis of how Hindu–Muslim riots in colonial India were used by the British to establish 'communal strife' as 'one of the most distinctive features of the Indian society, past and present' (*SS VI* 132). In 'The Colonial Construction of

"Communalism": British Writings on Banaras in the Nineteenth Century' (1989), published in the sixth volume of *Subaltern Studies*, Pandey observes how the communal riot narrative was constructed and popularised by the British officials who were obsessed with the ethnic and doctrinal signs of the rival crowds. The administration, in the 1920s, drew up an elaborate list of Hindu–Muslim riots that had occurred in the country in the recent past, thereby deeply indoctrinating the discourse of difference and conflict as an inheritance from the past, into the collective memory of the nation. Gramsci's observations related to the history of religion in Europe suggest that the history of religion is constituted by two opposed tendencies – an attempt to formulate a universal moral code for the society on the one hand, and the struggle by the subjugated to resist the dominating implications of this code, on the other. In the context of a multi-religious nation like India, with two dominant sections of faith, these mutual conflicts – which might involve religious implications but are not restricted to differences in religious opinions alone – are more often than not ascribed to 'the centuries' old smouldering fire of communal strife' and thus justified as 'the politics of the indigenous community' (168).

The narrative of communalism in post-Independence India reached its climax with the Ram Janmabhoomi Movement in the 1980s. Surprisingly, women played an active role in providing leadership and mobilising this movement. In her essay titled 'The Woman as Communal Subject: Rashtrasevika Samiti and Ram Janmabhoomi Movement', published in the *Economic and Political Weekly* in August 1991, Tanika Sarkar brings together the two different strands of gender and religion in a comprehensive sociological survey of the movement. She analyses how the Ram Janmabhoomi Movement highlights the role of the woman as a *karsevika* (religious volunteer) who 'stepped out of a purely iconic status to take up active position as a militant'. By using the family as a metaphor of functionality, the RSS (Rashtriya Swayamsevak Sangh) – the parent organisation – mobilised women through training provided by community-based organisations, while accepting and celebrating their gender roles, and emphasising their 'Hindu' identity. Sarkar presents the complexity of the situation as she observes that in terms of feminist liberation, the movement helped 'hitherto homebound women to reclaim public spaces' and conferred upon them 'a political role and even leadership'. However, by highlighting their gender identity within a religious context of pre-planned political agenda, it initiates these women into a public identity which is 'regimented, colourless, grim', and makes them part of 'a violent campaign of blind hatred' and not a 'critique of class, caste and patriarchy' (Sarkar, 'The Woman as Communal Subject' 2062).

Reiterating the complexities associated with gender identity in the sociopolitical domain of post-Independence India, in the 1990s, Susie Tharu and Tejaswini Niranjana engage in a detailed study of women's participation and visibility in their essay 'Problems for a Contemporary Theory of Gender' (1996), published in the ninth volume of *Subaltern Studies*. They observe that an analysis of gender as a marker of identity shows how the 'humanist subject and the social worlds predicated onto it' function in a manner so as to 'legitimize bourgeois and patriarchal interests' (*SS IX* 235). They argue that the techniques of analysis employed by Marxist or feminist approaches which take into consideration the other hidden structures of subjugation for the woman as a subject, such as caste and community, do not form a part of the dominant discourse. Therefore, at the social level, there is no effective critique of the inequalities of caste or community implicit in the functioning of the woman as a subaltern subject. Instead, the focus seems to have shifted to 'hegemonic mobilizations of a "feminist" subject' specific to the times (260).

Ranajit Guha observes in his essay titled 'The Small Voice of History' (1996), included in the ninth volume, that the study of history was introduced by the British in nineteenth-century India with its roots in institutionalised knowledge and statist perspectives. He argues that this innate statism, which is the contribution of Western education, has been a defining characteristic of Indian history even in the postcolonial times. The myriad voices of the civil society which form the actual history of the nation are 'drowned in the noise of statist commands' (*SS IX* 3). Guha proposes the objective of Subaltern Studies to be directed towards the emergence of a 'new historiography sensitized to the undertones of despair and determination' which will 'overthrow the regime of bourgeois narratology' (12).

This vision of an alternative history voicing the subaltern existence was realised globally when the approach of Subaltern Studies was adopted in Latin America with the formation of the Latin American Subaltern Studies Group in 1993. The scope, vision and range of this collective will be discussed in the fifth chapter. Connecting the South Asian initiative and the Latin American project in the essay 'Subaltern Studies: Projects for Our Time and Their Convergence' (1996), Ranajit Guha writes that 'it is not territoriality that relates our project to theirs in a bond of mutual relevance, but temporality' (*The Small Voice of History* 347). This convergence of the two collectives across two distinct spatio-temporal contexts and against two distinct historical backgrounds, hints at a collapse of local and global times. Though the contexts which gave rise to the Subaltern Studies Collective in India did not hold valid for Latin America, the historical narrative of subjugation was equally applicable in the latter case and therefore, provided the ground for adopting a similar perspective to rediscover the drowned 'small' voices of history in a completely altered space and time. Guha acknowledges postmodernism as the basis of this conjunction and declares that both the collectives would strive to 'unshackle the critique of reason from its tutelage to statism' (360).

In fact, this collapse of space and time with reference to the perspective of Subaltern Studies may be seen to be apparent in the tenth volume published by the group in 1999. Apart from essays analysing subalternity in Indian contexts, it also includes studies which map subaltern articulations through the plight of Indian indentured labourers in Fiji and the conditions of women in Palestine. In the essay 'Diaspora and the Difficult Art of Dying', Sudesh Mishra traces the overlapping of history and memory as he provides a detailed account of displacement, disillusionment, loss of identity and a yearning for a long-lost homeland through the perspective of the *girmitiyas* who had left India as indentured labourers. He notes, 'India slipped through my fingers like silk, like silk it slipped through the fingers of three-thousand-seven-hundred-

and-forty-eight girmitiyas, and many things were lost during that nautical passage' (*SS X* 2). Similarly, in 'Gendering the "Nationalist Subject": Palestinian Camp Women's Life Stories', Rosemary Sayigh asserts the need to 'conceptualize a female nationalist subject whose narrations have multiple values: re-historicizing the home, gender, and sexuality; outlining the contours of 'indigenous feminisms' through anecdotes of daily life struggles' (*SS X* 236).

With its thrust on critiquing subjugation, the Subaltern Studies Collective expanded its study of subalternisation from the domains of class to include caste and religion. The twelfth and final volume of *Subaltern Studies*, published in 2005, is titled 'Muslims, Dalits and the Fabrications of History'. It explores how the politics of majoritarian groups create fabricated narratives of the past in order to endorse a futuristic vision of homogenised history, by obliterating caste and religious identities. Shahid Amin, in 'Representing the Musalman: Then and Now, Now and Then', examines how 'the descriptive phrase "India has a majority of Hindus" has now been fashioned into the battering ram of Hindu nationalism' whose aim is to 'enforce the majoritarian idea of a singular national history' (*SS XII* 1). Amin observes that the chief instrument of this propagandist vision of aggressive Hindu nationalism is 'the enactment of historical vendetta against the Muslim conquest of pre-colonial India' which then serves as the condition 'demarcating the "natural" citizens of India' (1). He provides a detailed survey of the symbols, images and cultural associations which construct the stereotype of the 'Musalman' in India through an analysis of popular cultural motifs used in posters, advertisements and billboards. For instance, he shows how the Turkish cap or the fez is repeatedly used as a visual marker for the 'Muslim' attire and observes that 'the Turkish cap as a marker of Muslim distinctiveness is in fact quite nonsensical' (5). However, Amin argues, such stereotypical images have been so integrated with the popular cultural imagination of the Muslim identity through a larger process of fabrication of the past, that a young citizen of India belonging to the Muslim community is easily perceived as the '*santaan of Babur*' (descendent of Babur) against whom the 'majoritarian Hindu' section of the population can exercise their right to take revenge, as 'heard during the *masjid-*

bhoomi turmoil' (10). Further, Amin provides a detailed semiotic study of the word 'Hindustani' with reference to various literary and non-literary works. He observes that 'in the post-Partition decades', the word 'Hindustani' stood for 'all North Indians/ Indians', and concludes with reference to a popular film song of the 1960s where the phrase 'Hum Hindustani' was used to 'evoke a New Age Nehruvian consensus' as an 'exhortation to non-sectarian nation-building' (35).

Similarly, caste as a component of subalternity is analysed by Milind Wakankar in his essay titled 'The Anomaly of Kabir: Caste and Canonicity in Indian Modernity', published in the twelfth volume. Deconstructing the popularity of Kabir, the fifteenth-century Indian saint–poet, in the present context, Wakankar writes that 'Kabir draws our attention to that recalcitrant strain in language' which serves as an 'untimely resource for the marginalized groups' such as the 'Untouchables, who describe themselves today as Dalits ("the downtrodden") and tribals' (*SS XII* 100). Situating the historical Kabir who describes himself as belonging to the Untouchables and the weaver community of Banaras, Wakankar asserts that 'the vocation of Bhakti was to introduce the idea of heterogeneity into the transcendentalized secularism of the *Gita*' (107). This 'detranscendentalisation' was achieved by Bhakti poets through the expression of local experience in vernacular languages to voice the marginalised. Wakankar observes that 'in the interstices of this chequered history of detranscendentalization', one can locate 'the mystery or secret of caste subalternity' (108). He argues that a caste-based critique of nationalist history 'attempts to recover from the historical and cultural mainstream of national culture the wherewithal for an autonomous Dalit tradition' (122).

THE DECLINE OF THE COLLECTIVE IN LATE 1990s

Towards the late 1990s, certain differences of opinion surfaced within the group that led to a gradual decline of the Subaltern Studies Collective. Though the last volume of *Subaltern Studies* was published in 2005, there had been questions about the validity and relevance of the decade-long journey of the Collective, and of the Subaltern Studies perspective, and about its conformity to and deviations from the original plan. A well-known critique of the perspective was offered by Sumit Sarkar, a former member of the group, in his essay 'The Decline of the Subaltern in *Subaltern Studies*', published in *Writing Social History* (1997). In this essay, Sarkar observes that the aims with which the group began its journey have undergone changes, and the present status of acclaim enjoyed by this approach is due to the 'Western academic postmodernistic counter-establishment which is interested in colonial and postcolonial matters' (84). He engages in a detailed delineation of the shift in perspective and cites how the reference to the struggles of the subaltern classes has declined in the later volumes published by the group. Instead, he argues, in the later volumes, the dominant thrust is on a critique of 'Western-colonial power-knowledge', and an alternative is proposed by a 'non-Western "community consciousness"', wherein such consciousness is defined 'principally in terms of religious identities' (82). Sarkar, therefore, claims that the analytical scope offered by the Group has diminished, given that it had initially emerged as a major voice of dissent countering the mainstream dominant narratives of power by acknowledging the heterogeneity of subaltern identities.

In *Postcolonial Theory and the Specter of Capital* (2013), Vivek Chibber critiques the approach adopted by the Subaltern Studies Project. He analyses the works of Ranajit Guha, Dipesh Chakrabarty and Partha Chatterjee to establish that the derivations of the widely popular Subaltern Studies approach centre around Eurocentrism, and that the approach is reductionist in nature. Chibber, therefore, argues that the foundational tenets of Subaltern Studies are based on a series of analytical and historical misinterpretations. Partha Chatterjee presents a counter-argument to Chibber's comments in his essay titled 'Subaltern Studies and *Capital*', published in *The Economic and Political Weekly* (14 September 2013). Chatterjee observes that Chibber misconstrues the implications of the works of these scholars and that his assertions are based on a 'gross misunderstanding of Guha's claims'. He dismisses Chibber's claim to a universal model which insists that 'capitalism or the struggles of subaltern classes must be the same everywhere'. Instead, Chatterjee claims that these struggles are heterogeneous in nature and that the historians of Subaltern Studies 'have only attempted to interpret a small part of these struggles' (75).

★★★

Subaltern Studies, as a postcolonial approach, has certainly provided new directions to the study and understanding of Indian history and society. By acknowledging the pluralities of perspectives permeating the domain of historiography, it has equipped scholars and researchers with a critical insight into the sweeping generalisations of mainstream bourgeois narratives. The remaining chapters in this book engage in a detailed analysis of subalternity through various markers of individual identity, such as caste, class, gender, space and the contemporary domains of ableist discourse.

REFERENCES

Amin, Shahid, and Dipesh Chakrabarty, ed. *Subaltern Studies IX: Writings on South Asian History and Society.* Oxford UP, 1996.

Bhadra, Gautam, Gyan Prakash, and Susie Tharu, ed. *Subaltern Studies X: Writings on South Asian History and Society.* Oxford UP, 1999.

Chatterjee, Partha. 'Subaltern Studies and "Capital"'. *Economic and Political Weekly* 48.37 (2013). 69–75. <http://www.jstor.org/stable/23528277>.

Chibber, Vivek. *Postcolonial Theory and the Specter of Capital.* Verso Books, 2013.

Gramsci, Antonio. *Selections from the Prison Notebooks.* International Publishers, 1971.

Guha, Ranajit, ed. *Subaltern Studies I: Writings on South Asian History and Society.* Oxford UP, 1982.

----, ed. *Subaltern Studies II: Writings on South Asian History and Society.* Oxford UP, 1983.

----, ed. *Subaltern Studies III: Writings on South Asian History and Society.* Oxford UP, 1984.

----, ed. *Subaltern Studies IV: Writings on South Asian History and Society.* Oxford UP, 1985.

----, ed. *Subaltern Studies V: Writings on South Asian History and Society*. Oxford UP, 1987.

----, ed. *Subaltern Studies VI: Writings on South Asian History and Society*. Oxford UP, 1989.

----. *The Small Voice of History*. Permanent Black, 2009.

Mayaram, Shail, M. S. S. Pandian, and Ajay Skaria, ed. *Subaltern Studies XII: Muslims, Dalits and the Fabrications of History*. Permanent Black, 2005.

Sarkar, Sumit. *Writing Social History*. Oxford UP, 1997.

Sarkar, Tanika. 'The Woman as Communal Subject: Rashtrasevika Samiti and Ram Janmabhoomi Movement'. *Economic and Political Weekly* 26.35 (1991). 2057–62. <http://www.jstor.org/stable/41498633>.

Chapter Three

Subaltern Studies and Postcolonialism

Postcolonialism, as a theoretical approach towards history, interrogates the validity of history as it is documented within the framework of colonial power hierarchies. However, even the so-called postcolonial documentation of history follows the patterns and standards set by the West. This perspective has been instrumental in transforming the understanding of power equations, and of assertions of identity, in the history of the world. Within the postcolonial discourse, elitist historiography claims a dominant position in the documentation of nationalist history. The existence and the voices of the subaltern are engulfed by the larger narrative of nationalist glory framed by the dominant groups within the territorial space defined as a nation. Subaltern Studies seeks to trace and reclaim the position of subaltern individuals and groups latent in the dominant narrative of postcolonial history.

SUBALTERN STUDIES HISTORIOGRAPHY AND THE COLONIAL SUBJECT

In his article titled 'Subaltern Studies and Postcolonial Historiography' (2000), Dipesh Chakrabarty provides a detailed insight into the connection between postcolonial historiography and Subaltern Studies. He acknowledges the apparent similarities between Subaltern Studies and its claim to rewriting history, and the European Marxist perspectives. However, he differentiates between the Subaltern Studies approach towards documentation and analysis of history, and the English tradition of writing 'history from below' as practised by British Marxist historians like E. P. Thompson and Eric Hobsbawm, stating that the difference between the two approaches lies in the fact that Subaltern Studies comprises a critique of the nation-form and interrogates the relationship between power and knowledge. While Hobsbawm's concept of 'pre-political' is based on the European understanding of 'political' as a derivative of power and capital, in the Indian context, power does not necessarily imply capital, and the term 'political' can yield multiple implications based on the social stratification.

Chakrabarty refers to Ranajit Guha's explanation of the term 'political' in the Indian context being a continuous merging of two distinct categories – that of legal governance on one hand, and legitimised patterns of dominance such as religion and caste, on the other. Thus separating capital and power as two distinct categories, Chakrabarty argues that the history of colonial modernity in India constituted the 'political' as a distinctively heteroglossic component – including a diversity of voices, discourses and points of view. This idea of the political is characterised by its plurality, and holds within itself different types of relations which may not, necessarily, form a homogenised whole. This definition problematises the identity of the subaltern in the Indian context, due to the plurality of components such as ethnicity, community, caste and gender, which constitute the social fabric of the country.

Since all forms of representation or narrativisation – from history to literature and films – adhere to a certain narrative structure, they may be interpreted and analysed from various perspectives to investigate the latent narrative beneath the apparent or dominant discourse, to reclaim subaltern voices. In her essay entitled 'Can the Subaltern Speak?' (1988), Gayatri Chakravorty Spivak observes that the subjecthood of the colonised subaltern is characterised by heterogeneity. Given the scope and expanse of Subaltern Studies, various critical perspectives have emerged in the Indian context, which explore this heterogeneity of colonised subaltern groups. As Subaltern Studies enlarge the domain of history by foregrounding the subject-position of the subaltern who had been embedded and occluded in mainstream historiography, it creates possibilities of facilitating that act of reading as an *active* engagement with texts and events – to enable the reader to determine the role and contribution of the subaltern in multiple contexts relating to the nation.

SUBALTERN CRITIQUE OF POSTCOLONIAL HISTORIES

As discussed in previous chapters, in adopting the term 'subaltern', and in acknowledging domains of hegemonic dominance of the privileged classes over oppressed classes, Subaltern Studies is influenced by the ideas of Antonio Gramsci. The notion of power being rooted in the class identity of individuals or groups, similarly, had its origin in Marxism, where class is a derivative of capital. Michel Foucault's concept of power/knowledge, signifying that power is constituted by sanctioned forms of knowledge, also comes into play as 'official' mainstream histories are interrogated by Subaltern Studies in order to locate the fissures and ruptures in the narrative structure, so as to retrieve the existence of subaltern individuals and groups. This critique of the apparent totality presented by the structured narrative of official history leads to Subaltern Studies assuming a poststructuralist stance. The project of locating the voice of the oppressed subaltern, in turn, brings Subaltern Studies closer to the concept of 'history from below' as propounded by British Marxist historians. However, Subaltern Studies, as a theoretical approach, does not remain bounded within the domains of these theories; it has evolved into a technique of reading postcolonial history against the grain.

With the attainment of political independence, the primary project for a newly developed nation is to rewrite its own history from a postcolonial perspective. This history is envisioned to provide a desirably harmonious image of a single unified nation, which might then be used to indoctrinate the politically subordinated individuals and groups with a sense of nationalism, constituting them as citizens of the nation. Subaltern Studies as a postcolonial approach begins from where these nationalist narratives of coherent histories end. It revisits these postcolonial histories, reading them against the grain, to mark out in the seemingly smooth flow of events, the ruptures which engulf episodes of struggle against the colonial rule carried out by indigenous groups of common people without acknowledgement or leadership from the colonised elite. The peasant uprisings in colonial India are a case in point.

The subaltern in the postcolonial context is not constituted in terms of class alone. For instance, the peasant is not subalternised only on the basis of class. There can be several markers of subaltern identity – such as caste, religion, race, region and gender, to name a few. The Marxist definition of the subjugated, therefore, in the context of postcolonialism, does not remain confined to the criteria of class. So, a simple appropriation of Marxist theory cannot suitably apply to the postcolonial state. Consequently, the concept of power also undergoes a paradigm shift. Power is no longer constituted by class and capital alone. Thus, the nature of authority within the social fabric giving rise to power equations comes to be determined by a heterogeneity of factors. Hence, the Foucauldian concept of power constituting knowledge and knowledge granting sanction to power, might have several other formulations in a postcolonial society.

The British Marxist historian E. P. Thompson, in his essay 'History from Below', published in the *Times Literary Supplement* in 1966, advocates the idea of rewriting history from the perspective of the common people. This re-exploration of the homogeneous narratives of elitist history proposes an alternative vision of history from the perspective of the common people. In the preface to *The Making of the English Working Class* (1963), Thompson claims, 'I am seeking to rescue the poor stockinger, the Luddite cropper, the "obsolete" hand-loom weaver, the "utopian" artisan, and even the deluded follower of Joanna Southcott, from the enormous condescension of posterity' (12). This concept of writing 'history from below' had a tremendous influence on Marxist scholars during the 1970s. Subaltern Studies, too, was influenced by this approach.

However, as elucidated by Dipesh Chakrabarty, in his article discussed briefly above, Subaltern historiography differs from 'history from below' broadly on three premises. Firstly, by conceptualising the subaltern as a heterogeneous entity, it underlines a separation of the history of power from the authoritative histories of capital.

Secondly, it brings the idea of the 'national' to crisis by critiquing the nation-form. Also, it calls for an alternative understanding of archival material since subaltern utterances cannot be found in the 'official' mainstream state archives. Consequently, Subaltern Studies finds its sources or archival material from the domains of anthropology, culture studies, literature, sociology, archaeology, demography, etc., and therefore becomes an intersectional area of cross-disciplinary examination. Therefore, thirdly and finally, in this manner Subaltern Studies engages in a critique of the relationship between power and knowledge, by questioning the validity of mainstream archives and thereby history itself as a form of knowledge.

In *Subaltern Studies II* (1983), Ranajit Guha classifies the corpus of historical writings on subaltern uprisings – in this case, peasant insurgencies – as constituted by primary, secondary and tertiary discourses. The primary range of discourse emerges from the official records and documents meant for administrative use and are located closest to the historicity of the incidents in terms of their immediacy. The secondary discourse is constituted by those archival documents which draw their raw material from primary sources, such as memoirs or administrative documents meant for a non-official readership. In these documents, the event is reported and analysed by the writer, thereby imparting a distinct perspective to the actual event, which is retrospective in nature. The secondary discourse, therefore, unlike the primary discourse, lacks the quality of instantaneousness with respect to the historicity of the event documented. Borrowing from Roland Barthes, Guha describes the difference between these two discourses as that between '*functions* and *indices*'. While the former comprises 'segments that make up a linear sequence of a narrative', the latter may be regarded as derivatives of micro-sequences from the former to which 'it should be possible to assign names by a metalinguistic operation', which may or may not belong to the original subject under consideration (Guha, *SS II* 10).

In this manner, the narrative of history itself becomes a subject of poststructuralist analysis where the unity of the apparent structure is challenged in the act of reading. Multiple versions of documents constituting the secondary discourse might disrupt the linearity of the primary discourse through continuous vertical interventions. Both these forms claim objectivity, but neither traces the rebel, who is the subaltern, as the subject of rebellion.

Unlike the first two discourses, the documents comprising the tertiary discourse about the subaltern are always written in the third person. They are non-official accounts which do not declare loyalty to any particular form of state power. The purpose of such accounts is to retrieve the history of the subaltern uprising and present them to the readers in an alternative axis of space and time. However, as Guha observes, as with colonialist historiographies, these attempts too amount 'to an act of appropriation which excludes the rebel as a conscious subject of his own history' (Guha, *SS II* 33). He cites the example of the efforts made by radical historians to retrieve subaltern narratives of peasant insurgencies in India. These historians could not, however, accept the religious sentiments that animated the subalterns in question and dismissed them as backwardness. Thus, the subaltern, denied of his/her beliefs, becomes a subject re-moulded by a liberalist and radical historical consciousness. The same holds true for the radical perceptions of historians guided by Western ideas regarding markers of subaltern identity which are peculiar to the Third World, particularly India, such as caste. The subject-position of the subaltern is compromised by denying them their own claims to rationality and logic. Such accounts are shaped by Western paradigms of modernity, politics, humanism and power.

None of these discourses generated around the subaltern, thus, succeed in portraying the subject-position of the subaltern to the readers. History fails itself and its purpose despite a complexity of narrative techniques employed, and Guha concludes that this is perhaps what makes historical discourse 'the world's oldest thriller' (Guha, *SS II* 10). Subaltern Studies, as an analytical approach to postcolonial histories, begins by acknowledging this impossibility of grasping completely a past consciousness and by abandoning the claim to reconstitute it. By reading postcolonial histories against their grain, Subaltern Studies can, at the most, claim to provide a close approximation of the subaltern consciousness.

Therefore, though Subaltern Studies is influenced by several Western theoretical and philosophical ideas, the praxis adopted by Subaltern Studies scholars is not a simple pastiche of blended theoretical approaches. It serves as a critique of the Western ideas it draws on, in the final point of view it adopts. In fact, in an essay titled 'Subaltern Studies as Postcolonial Criticism' (1994), Gyan Prakash asserts that 'Subaltern Studies obtains its force as postcolonial criticism from a catachrestic combination of Marxism, Poststructuralism, Gramsci and Foucault, the modern West and India, archival research and textual criticism' (17). 'Catachresis' here refers to Derrida's concept of deconstruction where the term is used to denote an essential incompleteness which is inherent in all systems of meaning.

POSTCOLONIALITY AND HISTORICAL PERSPECTIVES

The term 'representation' presupposes the allotment of a subject-position to the individual or group being represented as a performative act of power by the narratorial authority. In case of historiography, the events represented attain a particular colour and character by virtue of the narratorial perspective. Under differing perspectives, therefore, the same historical event as a 'text' may yield completely different readings.

In the postcolonial context, an interesting example of this may be seen in the writing of narratives related to the Uprising of 1857. Since the 'official' historical accounts of India under the colonial regime were written and maintained by the coloniser, in the beginning of the twentieth century and with the rise of the nationalist consciousness, the need for altering the perspective on the Uprising was felt. Hence, there was a marked shift in the description of the Uprising of 1857 in postcolonial historiographies, when compared to John Kaye's *A History of the Sepoy War in India* (1857–58) or G. B. Malleson's *History of the Indian Mutiny* (1878–80). One of the earliest texts from an Indian perspective, and voicing this need for a shift in perspective, was *The Indian War of Independence 1857* (1907) by Vinayak Damodar Savarkar who wrote, 'The nation ought to be the master and not the slave of its own history' (ix). The use of the master–slave equation here refers to the act of writing history. By asserting that the nation ought to be the master of its own history, Savarkar calls for a change of perspective – from that of the coloniser to that of the colonised – and the assumption of an active role by the colonised, in the wake of the rise of the nationalist consciousness in the early twentieth century. Though the actual events in historical time and space remain stable, what changes with the shifting axes of time and perspective is the manner in which the events of the past are interpreted. In his book published to mark the golden jubilee of the historical event, thus, Savarkar re-explores the Uprising of 1857 and notes how it upholds the spirit of 'a War of Independence' (Savarkar ix). The necessity to integrate the colonially subjugated under an integrated banner of nationalism led to a semiotic shift in the reading of what was recorded as a 'mutiny' by the coloniser as a 'War of Independence'.

Time yields perspectives. After the attainment of political independence at the cost of Partition, in 1957, the Government of India celebrated the centenary of the Uprising of 1857. In his preface to the book titled *Eighteen Fifty-Seven* by Surendra Nath Sen, published to mark the occasion, Maulana Abul Kalam Azad pointed out that there were no accounts of this great historical event from the Indian point of view, and therefore emphasised 'the need of writing a new history of the great uprising of 1857, generally described as the Sepoy Mutiny' (Sen x). Azad's proposal to initiate a change of perspective is different from Savarkar's. In the new postcolonial context, the same historical event now held in itself the popular instance of a people's movement spreading across religions – and a message of communal harmony which was, in the new context, much needed for the smooth functioning of a newly formed democracy. In fact, this becomes more obvious when one reads Pandit Jawaharlal Nehru in his documentation of the Revolt of 1857 in *Glimpses of World History* (1934): 'it had no good leadership; it was badly organized, and there were mutual squabbles all the time' (480). However, after Independence, the celebration of the centenary of the Uprising of 1857 as a nationalist movement was organised by the Government of India with Nehru himself at the helm as prime minister.

In the same year, P. C. Joshi, who was General Secretary of the Communist Party of India till 1947, in his essay titled '1857 in Our History', read the Uprising from a Marxist perspective and wrote, 'there were other social forces of the common people in action during this struggle and they had brought new factors and ideas into play' (Joshi 137, 196–97). He critiques Nehru's perspective for having 'given no thought nor weight' to the common people involved in the Uprising (137). The shift in perspective in case of historiography, therefore, is necessitated by the changing axis of time and development of new sociopolitical and intellectual paradigms. To Joshi, the common people of India comprise the section subalternised by the Nehruvian documentation of the history of the Uprising, which is elitist in nature. The same historical event, thus, becomes a text to be interpreted to yield new meanings, despite its historical specificity.

With the passage of time and the emergence of Subaltern Studies as a postcolonial approach in the 1980s, historians felt the need to re-read and re-analyse history to understand the subjugated colonised as the silenced subaltern. When perceived as a mass movement, the Uprising of 1857, as a historical event, holds within itself the potential to yield multiple histories of people rendered invisible and denied their space by erstwhile historians. Such readings and analysis unearth localised legends and fables which are hitherto unheard of. One such case is that of Baba Ramsanehi, as recorded by Amritlal Nagar in his book *Ghadar ke phool* (1982). In the book, the legend of Baba Ramsanehi – a name lost to the mainstream histories of 1857 but whose *samadhi* continues to be revered by the locals even after a hundred years of the Uprising – is described at length. While mainstream historiography highlights the major events led by elitist political ideologies, Subaltern Studies unearths local events headed by the masses.

In his *A History of Indian Literature 1800–1910; Western Impact: Indian Response* (1991), Sisir Kumar Das acknowledges the presence of oral literature as a means of archiving reactions towards different events affecting lives of the common people within the context of a colonised nation. Such oral narratives continue to exist and form a flow of tradition alternative to the mainstream approaches constituting knowledge. However, these two streams, when they engage with each other, give rise to a new kind of historical archive in the form of literature. For instance, Indranath Choudhuri notes in his essay 'Tradition of folk in Literature' that 'the folk *allahas* of Madhya Pradesh inspired the Hindi poetess Subhadra Kumari Chauhan to write her famous poem "Khub lari mardani vaha tou Jhansivali rani thi"' (03). While these original folk *allahas* may no longer be retrievable in their entirety, the poem which gained popularity in the context of early–twentieth-century Indian nationalism is still a widely read piece across India.

The subaltern had, hence, existed through representations and oblique references long before the emergence of Subaltern Studies as an academic approach. This academic approach later formalised the domain as part of an accepted intellectual discourse. With subalternity emerging as a possible means of revisiting representations, a new critical perspective was developed for the study and analysis of latent, counter-hegemonic discourses in the otherwise established canon of historical studies. Sites of rupture from within the dominant structured narrative presented themselves for investigation and research, to rethink presence, absence and marginalisation. Existing critical approaches merged with Subaltern Studies to identify and locate more groups and individuals within the praxis of subalternity, in the larger domain of postcolonial studies.

For instance, in the context of the 1857 Uprising, the feminist critical approach led to a surge in the critique and re-exploration of the life of Rani Lakshmibai as a gendered participant in the historical event. Her life, her role in the rebellion, her transgression of the gender stereotype and representations of the same in history and literature, were studied with renewed interest. Further, with the rise of Dalit nationalism in the 1990s, Matadin Bhangi (Matadin Valmiki) – the untouchable who was refused a mug of water by Mangal Pandey due to his caste – came to be credited as the initiator of the Uprising. As D. C. Dinkar notes in his *Swatantrata sangram mein achhuton ka yogdan* (The Untouchables' Contribution to the Struggle for Freedom, 1990), it was Bhangi who then revealed to Pandey the truth about the cartridges, which in turn led to the Uprising at Barrackpore. In 'Reactivating the Past: Dalits and

Memories of 1857' (2007), Badri Narayan Tiwari observes that 'the dalits, through their narratives of 1857, have not only tried to establish their own heroes, but also tried to dethrone the existing high-caste heroes from the mainstream narratives' (Web, n.p.). Dalit feminist inquiries into the Uprising have similarly led to the emergence of new historical women martyrs such as Jhalkaribai, Udadevi, Aavantibai and Mahaviridevi.

Postcolonialism, therefore, with the emergence of Subaltern Studies, has become a site for contesting accepted elitist narratives and mainstream perspectives. Gyan Prakash, for instance, has traced the Western influence in the documentation of history. He states that in relocating the subaltern within the operation of dominant discourses, Subaltern Studies, mandatorily, leads to a critique of the modern West which is identified as 'a powerful entity created by a historical process that authorized it as the home of Reason, Progress and Modernity' (Prakash 1485). Subaltern Studies in the postcolonial context, aims at interrogating hegemonic mainstream documentations by problematising such identifications of 'Reason, Progress and Modernity' and unearthing the possible pluralities which lie latent within such identifications.

SUBALTERNITY IN POSTCOLONIAL LITERATURE

Postcolonial literature, primarily, engages with the representation of lives, times and events from the perspectives of the colonised. Subalternity in postcolonial literature is constituted by the representation of people who are marginalised – it engages in a fictional re-presentation of their points of view, their lives, and their stories. It explores how subalternity of individual or collective identity is constructed and perpetuated in postcolonial societies. In postcolonial literature, characters representing the people who are subalternised on the basis of caste, class, gender, ethnicity, race or an amalgamation of more than one such markers of identity, inhabit the plot as plausible marginalised presences at a given point of time. The narration sometimes involves references to the colonial phase in order to highlight the haplessness of the oppressed even in a politically independent nation. The individual lives of these characters emerge as voices of the subaltern waiting to be heard in the interstices of historical time. Their experiences, their joys and sorrows within the microcosm of their individual existence, enact the saga of silenced voices struggling against elitist homogenisation. As Homi Bhabha observes, 'these spheres of life are linked through an "in-between" temporality that takes the measure of dwelling at home, while producing an image of the world of history' (19).

An interesting example of this is provided by Salman Rushdie's novel *Midnight's Children* (1980). Narrated by the protagonist Saleem Sinai, the novel may be read as an allegory of the nation told through the lives of the children who were born on the day and at the hour when India attained political independence. Recollecting his birth which coincided with the moment of India's independence, Saleem says, 'I had been mysteriously handcuffed to history, my destinies indissolubly chained to those of my country' (Rushdie 9). Saleem, an illegitimate child of a Hindu woman and a British man, is raised in an affluent Muslim family, because his name tag was swapped by Mary Pereira with that of another child – later named Shiva – after his birth. This act reflects the vulnerable destinies forged by the hands of those in power – in this case Mary, who is driven by the Communist ideologies of Joseph D'Costa and wants to do her share by bringing a comfortable life to a child belonging to the underprivileged class. As a result of Mary's actions, Saleem grows up in a rich family, while Shiva – the original child of the Aziz family – is subjected to the harshness of poverty and violence. Saleem's identity is therefore representative of the inherent plurality and hybridity that characterises India.

In endowing the children born in India on the day of Independence with special powers, Rushdie employs the magic realist mode of writing to highlight the irony of the gifted existence of the one thousand and one children born in India on that day, against the dismal situations they go through in the course of the political events shaping the destiny of India as a nation. Interestingly, the children who are born closest to the stroke of midnight are supposed to be blessed with the most unique powers. Hence, Saleem and Shiva – both born at the stroke of midnight – have the special powers of telepathy and war, respectively. Saleem's power is in his nose, while Shiva's power is in his knees. The characters use their respective powers as the narrative unfolds. Saleem finds the other 'midnight's children' through his power of telepathy and arranges for a 'midnight's children conference'. There is a continuous tension between Saleem and Shiva as both want to claim supremacy within the group. They form an antithesis to one another. As Saleem's fortunes take a steep bend downward, Shiva who had a terrible childhood amidst poverty and deprivation, emerges as the victor an becomes 'India's most decorated war hero' (486).

While tracing Saleem's life as he moves from affluence to economic hardships as a commoner, Rushdie uses the narrative of India's journey as a nation through the various political events that took place after Independence as a continuous subtextual reference. The story narrated by Saleem – the subaltern narrator – is entangled with the larger history of the nation that he belongs to: his displacements, his immigration to various cities, his political involvements during the period of national Emergency, and his life as a political prisoner. Every event in his life is, in turn, representative of narratives of suppressed subaltern voices, whose lives are subsumed in the larger narrative of a homogeneous nation. The fragmented postmodernist technique of narration used by Rushdie is typically suggestive of the markers of catachrestic moments amidst the coalescing semiotics of individual memory and collective history. Just as the 'midnight's children' are all rounded up and deprived of their powers in the forced sterilisation camps during the Emergency, the promise of magic which the nation had started off with, is also lost. The magic associated with the day of Indian Independence is put to its end. This is poignantly uttered by Saleem towards the end, as he says, '... the offspring of Independence were not all human. Violence, corruption, poverty, generals, chaos, greed and pepperpots ... I had to go into exile to learn that the children of midnight were more varied than I' (405).

If *Midnight's Children* represents subalternity based on class, Arundhati Roy's *The God of Small Things* (1997) voices subalternity based on caste and gender. Set in Kerala, the novel narrates the story of Ammu and her children, Estha and Rahel. Ammu is treated by her society and her family as an outcaste for violating the norms of gender and the caste hierarchy. She is subjected to gender discrimination from her childhood as her father Pappachi denies her opportunity to get higher education, while her brother Chacko is sent to Oxford University. Marriage for Ammu is a means to escape ill-treatment at the hands of Pappachi. However, she suffers gender violence after marriage too, as her alcoholic husband beats her and even asks her to satisfy his boss in order to serve his interests. The body of the woman, therefore, is transformed into a property to be possessed or potential capital to be exploited when needed, at the hands of the husband whom patriarchy gives the power to dominate the wife. As Ammu escapes and returns to her village with her two children, she is socially ostracised and treated like a burden by her family, because in a patriarchal society marriage as a social institution commands complete submission and docility from the woman. In stepping out of her marital home, Ammu is guilty of violating the prevalent gender order.

Ammu finds a companion in Velutha. But she transgresses her gender role as well as casteist traditions of her society by falling in love with Velutha, the untouchable, and by claiming sexual agency. Roy here traces the historical narrative of conversion to Christianity during the British rule. The oppressed castes had embraced Christianity as a means of escaping the subjugation induced by the caste system. However, the irony was that soon after conversion, 'they were made to have separate churches and separate priests', and later after Independence, 'they were not entitled to any Government benefits like job reservations' because, technically, Christianity is casteless (Roy 74). This shows how subalterns like Velutha are rendered invisible by the decision makers, and cannot escape the exploitation at the hands of the power hierarchies, despite an apparent shift in power at the political level. Velutha, who does not succumb to the hegemonic order of caste identity, is finally beaten to death by the police. Althusser observes, in *Ideology and Ideological State Apparatuses* (1970), that the police are a form of the 'repressive state apparatus'. When Velutha is beaten ruthlessly in the police lockup, the political and social apparatuses merge to obliterate the individual identity of the subaltern. In the process, it becomes an instance of state-sanctioned violence silencing the voice of the subaltern. At the macro level, similar strategies of silencing subaltern insurgencies are adopted by the state almost universally. Subalternity in *The God of Small Things* finds expression at various levels through the lives of its different characters. For instance, Mammachi – Ammu's mother – is also a victim of gender violence. She is beaten and ill-treated by her husband, and later her son Chacko deprives her of her economic agency by taking over the pickle factory. Mammachi, thus, is another gendered subaltern whose life constitutes a narrative of constant and layered violence within the social unit of family. Similarly, the twins – Estha and Rahel – inherit subalternity, and the associated silence and helplessness, since their childhood. Bearing a hybrid religious identity by virtue of their birth – since their father is a Hindu and their mother a Syrian Christian – their social identity is problematised from childhood. They also find themselves to be unwanted in Ammu's maternal home because their mother had separated from her husband and thereby defied patriarchal norms of the society.

With the death of Ammu, the twins are separated as Estha is sent back to his father and Rahel remains alone in Ayemenem. This leads to lasting scars being incurred by both the characters which define their existence. Their childhood and the decisions regarding their fate, imposed upon them by the adults, portray the children as constituting a major but latent subaltern category who are denied all agency and voice. The trauma of separation manifests itself in the form of behavioural changes that the twins go through – Estha stops talking, while Rahel is thrice expelled from her school. After her marriage, Rahel proves to be a misfit in her marital relationship, and her 'emptiness' and inner chaos is described through her eyes which 'behaved as though they belonged to someone else' (Roy 19). The subjective identity of the silenced subaltern being continuously subjugated by various dominant power structures results in the configuring of a confused, fragmented self which can neither comprehend totality, nor define lack.

Subalternity, therefore, emerges as a complex area of exploration in postcolonial literature, and the articulation of subalternity in these literary works is diverse and multilayered. Just as the criteria constituting subalternity may be varied, in terms of different markers of individual identity, such as class, caste, gender, race, community, religion, ethnicity, or physical ability, the treatment of subalternity in postcolonial literature undergoes ideological shifts with reference to the component of subalternity being represented. What remains constant, however, is the terrain of interdisciplinary research that it presents to the readers. For instance, a representation or analysis of subalternity in any society calls for a historical knowledge of that society, so as to trace the utterance of the subaltern in literary representations against the socio-historic background of the nation or community. Further, the different components of marginalisation that constitute the subaltern as the subject may be analysed from various theoretical perspectives. Hence, it becomes mandatory for the student/researcher to be able to locate and disentangle these blended narratives of subjugation.

★★★

In the postcolonial world order, with the establishment of nation states, and the formulation of concepts of legal equality and civil rights, locating subalternity is a complex process. Enshrouded in egalitarian claims and reassuring proclamations of national progress, the characteristic defining subalternity in the postcolonial existence is, primarily, its apparent invisibility. While locating the voice of the subaltern in the fissures of postcolonial historiography involves a critique of the nation's colonised past, studying subalternity within postcolonial societies initiates a process of unravelling an ongoing politics of silencing marginalised voices by power hierarchies. Nations formulate their own logic to perpetuate the process of subalternisation of people and groups who do not fit into the larger homogenised narratives of national glory. Gyanendra Pandey notes that 'difference' is 'the mark of the subordinated or subalternised, precisely because it is measured against the purported mainstream', and that, 'it is in the attribution of difference that the logic of dominance and subordination has always found expression' (4740). In the context of India, an important example may be seen in the case of Kashmir. The region and its inhabitants are often occluded from the national narratives of progress because, constitutionally and historically, they are seen to articulate a difference. This difference becomes the basis of a sustained process of subalternisation.

Consequently, the rights of the people of the region, their lives and livelihood are often kept outside the domains of nationalist discourse. Similarly, the northeastern states of India are usually understood in terms of the difference they represent in terms of the physical features of the people of the region, and their ethnicities and cultures. Their relationship with the 'main land' of India is hence dominated by this articulation of difference – leading to a homogenisation of these states and terming them collectively as the 'seven sister states'. These issues have been discussed at length in the eighth chapter. Thus, it is in the ruptures in the dominant narratives of the nation state that one may locate voices of the subaltern. For instance, within the fissures of a professed secularism one may find the narrative of subalternisation on the basis of religion, while within the gaps of the dominant discourse on gender equality may lie the story of subalternisation on the basis of gender.

REFERENCES

Amin, Shahid, and Dipesh Chakrabarty, ed. *Subaltern Studies IX: Writings on South Asian History and Society*. Oxford UP, 1996.

Bhabha, Homi. *The Location of Culture*. Routledge, 1994.

Chakrabarty, Dipesh. 'Subaltern Studies and Postcolonial Historiography'. *Nepantla: Views from South* 1.1 (2000): 9–32. <muse.jhu.edu/article/23873>.

Chatterjee, Partha, and Gyanendra Pandey, ed. *Subaltern Studies VII: Writings on South Asian History and Society*. Oxford UP, 1992.

Choudhuri, Indranath. 'Traditions of folk in Literature'. <http://www.indranathchoudhuri.com/Articles%20new%20new/3/Traditions%20of%20folk%20in%20Literature.pdf>.

Dinkar, D. C. *Swatantrata Sangram mein Achhuton ka Yogdan*. Bodhisatva Prakashan, 1990.

Guha, Ranajit, ed. *Subaltern Studies I: Writings on South Asian History and Society*. Oxford UP, 1982.

----, ed. *Subaltern Studies II: Writings on South Asian History and Society*. Oxford UP, 1983.

----, ed. *Subaltern Studies III: Writings on South Asian History and Society*. Oxford UP, 1984.

----, ed. *Subaltern Studies IV: Writings on South Asian History and Society.* Oxford UP, 1985.

----, ed. *Subaltern Studies V: Writings on South Asian History and Society.* Oxford UP, 1987.

----, ed. *Subaltern Studies VI: Writings on South Asian History and Society.* Oxford UP, 1989.

Hobsbawm, E. J. *Primitive Rebels.* Abacus, 2017.

Joshi, P.C. ed. *Rebellion 1857.* National Book Trust, 2007.

Marx, Karl, and Friedrich Engels. *The Communist Manifesto.* Lernert Publishing Group, 2018.

Nagar, Amritlal. *Ghadar Ke Phool.* Rajpal and Sons Publishing, 2011.

Nehru, Jawaharlal. *Glimpses of World History.* Penguin Books, 2004.

Pandey, Gyanendra. 'The Subaltern as Subaltern Citizen'. *Economic and Political Weekly* 41.46 (2006): 4735–41. JSTOR, <www.jstor.org/stable/4418914>.

Prakash, Gyan. 'Subaltern Studies as Postcolonial Criticism'. *The American Historical Review* 99.5 (1994): 1475–90. JSTOR, <www.jstor.org/stable/2168385>.

Roy, Arundhati. *The God of Small Things.* Penguin, 2002.

Rushdie, Salman. *Midnight's Children.* Vintage Books, 2008.

Savarkar, V. D. *The Indian War of Independence 1857.* Rajdhani Granthagar, 1970.

Sen, Surendra Nath. *Eighteen Fifty-Seven.* Publications Division, 1957.

Spivak, Gayatri Chakravorty. 'Can the Subaltern Speak?'. *Literary Theory: An Introductory Reader.* Ed. Saugata Bhaduri and Simi Malhotra. Anthem Press, 2010.

Thompson, E.P. *The Making of the English Working Class.* <https://uncomradelybehaviour.files.wordpress.com/2012/04/thompson-ep-the-making-of-the-english-working-class.pdf>

Tiwari, Badri Narayan. 'Reactivating the Past: Dalits and Memories of 1857'. *Economic and Political Weekly* 42.19 (2007): 1734–38. JSTOR, <www.jstor.org/stable/4419578>.

Chapter Four

Subaltern Studies and Postcolonial Feminism

THE GENDERED SUBALTERN

Gender, as a social construct, creates a binaristic segregation of the society. From the distinction between 'male' and 'female', social acculturation generates predetermined categories of heteronormative gender codes labelled as 'masculine' and 'feminine'. Patriarchy sanctions dominance of the masculine over the feminine, thereby leading to the birth of feminism that seeks social and political equality. Having started off towards the end of the eighteenth century and continuing into the nineteenth century as a social movement, primarily seeking legal and political rights for women, feminism gradually developed into an intellectual discourse in the first half of the twentieth century, mostly with the European white woman as the subject. It was led and defined by a homogenous conceptualisation of the category called 'women' and was largely represented by Anglo-American and French critics and theoreticians.

Towards the second half of the twentieth century, however, feminism, as a theoretical approach, diversified to recognise the needs of women as a heterogeneous community. This was triggered by the experiences of African-American women who were subjugated in terms of race as well as gender, and also the comparatively recent experience of the Second World War where women were engaged in the War as active workforce but were, once the War ended, expected to return to their homes and prioritise domesticity. These diversities of contexts and lives led to a diversified understanding of womanhood and the experiences associated with it, thereby opening up feminism to interdisciplinary approaches. The second half of the twentieth century also witnessed the emergence of postcolonialism as an academic perspective, which, in turn, added to the complexity of the category called 'women' by including within its purview the lives and contexts of Asian and Third World women.

The needs and concerns of European white women no longer dominated the discursive domain of feminism. It emerged as a plural concept aimed at addressing the needs of women across cartographic demarcations. These needs came to be defined by geographical, traditionalist and ethnocentric norms of subjugation under patriarchy. Hence, feminism, towards the end of the twentieth century, emerged as an area embodying the claims of equality which are specific to different categories of women with reference to their geospatial and cultural realities.

In the context of Subaltern Studies, feminism serves as another possible criterion of locating the subaltern. The woman, from this perspective, emerges as the 'gendered subaltern' who is subjected to different levels of oppression based on her gender as well as her class and caste. Within the larger matrix of her existence, she is construed as an individual belonging to the 'Second Sex' and hence is dominated by patriarchal norms. However, simultaneously, she is also the recipient of oppression based on her caste, class race and such multiple layers of hierarchies. Moreover, within her own community or class she is further dominated by the patriarchal order of her immediate society. Therefore, the woman, as the gendered subaltern, is doubly marginalised. She is rendered voiceless by such diverse parameters of subjugation. The subaltern historian or researcher seeks to disentangle these dominant tapestries of hierarchical apparatus to retrieve the subjectivity and utterance of the woman as the gendered subaltern.

FEMINISMS' EXPANDING HORIZONS

The first and second waves of feminisms were restricted in their scope and sought to identify and address the needs and concerns of the European white woman. Despite the participation of women of colour in the suffrage movement, African-American women did not feature in the dominant discourses of feminism through the first half of the twentieth century, which assumed a monistic identification of the woman's identity without considering the differences. Similarly, the European mainstream feminist discourse failed to comprehend the plurality of subject-positions associated with Third World women – governed by multiple factors such as caste and class, which made their situation very different from that of their European counterparts. Ironically, despite the gradual developments in feminist theories expanding in their scope to include socialist, Marxist and postmodern approaches to feminism, the basic visible differences remained unrecognised – such as those of race, class and caste. This led to the emergence of different groups of feminists addressing diverse contexts and acknowledging the different subject-positions of women who are doubly marginalised, thereby making feminism a plural concept.

Black Feminism/African-American Feminism

Towards the 1950s, the civil rights movement began in America. African-American men as well as women participated in it to claim racial equality. However, even within the movement, the important positions were occupied by African-American men, asserting a patriarchal hierarchy within the community, while the women were thought of as people supporting their men in their struggle for equal rights in this movement against racism. African-American women were, therefore, subjected to a process of double-marginalisation, where they were oppressed outside their communities on the grounds of their racial identity and for their gender, and within their communities, on the basis of gender. Their subject-hood, thus constituted, was very different from that of white European women, who by this time, had gained their political rights and for whom feminism was at this point, more about the subtler issues of male dominance. This invisibility of the African-American woman as a subject of Eurocentric feminist discourse and the resultant denial of her voice led to the emergence of African-American feminism where the women belonging to the African American community voiced their subject-position, and their marginalisation by racism and sexism.

Sojourner Truth's (1797–1883) speech at the Women's Convention held at Ohio in 1851, which put forth an important question on behalf of all African-American women – 'ain't I a woman?' – re-emerged with the discontent and disillusionment offered by the civil rights movement and Eurocentric feminism, and led to the emergence of African-American feminism or Black feminism in the 1960s and 70s. In 1970, the *Black Women's Manifesto* was published by the Third World Women's Alliance, which highlighted the distinctive nature of oppression faced by the women belonging to the African-American community. Arpita Mukhopadhyay observes that 'the agenda of black feminists was to establish their identity against patriarchy in their culture, and the models established by the mainstream feminists' (83).

In *Ain't I A Woman: Black Women and Feminism* (1981), bell hooks (Gloria Watkins) provides a detailed history of African-American women and traces their subjugation from the times of slavery to the late-twentieth century at the hands of racism and sexism. She asserts that racism and sexism are intertwined and cannot be addressed as compartmentalised realities as far as these African-American women are concerned. Right from the period of slave trade and the ill treatment of women on the ships, hooks notes, 'rape was a common method of torture slavers used to subdue recalcitrant black women' (18). She traces how the Black woman as a slave served multiple requirements of the white master's household – as breeder, wet nurse, nanny, household help, and sometimes, in the plantations, as a 'surrogate male'. The beginning of the nineteenth century in America saw the emergence of the image of the white woman 'mythologized as pure and virtuous' and consequently the Black woman was construed as diametrically opposite – the one who could be easily sexually violated (hooks 31). hooks notes, 'as American white men idealised white womanhood, they sexually assaulted and brutalized black women' (32). They were perceived by white men as readily available sexual objects, and white women looked down upon the Black woman as a seductress or temptress, symbolic of sexual bestiality.

This systematic degradation of Black womanhood and continuous alienation from the mainstream which materially deprived them of their right over their lives and rendered them sexually vulnerable, continued even as slavery ended. Sexism was predominant even within the Black community and patriarchal values advocating male supremacy were embedded into the Black communities by the white racist oppressors. Hence, while on the one hand, Black women were negatively comprehended by white men and women, Black men also imposed upon them patriarchal gender roles and behaviour.

The twentieth century saw the emergence of many organisations and Black cultural movements. The National Association for the Advancement of Colored People (NAACP) was formed in 1909. The Harlem Renaissance, also known as the New Negro Movement, which began in the 1920s and continued till the 30s, was an assertion of a new identity by the Blacks and was a major counter-narrative offered by a subterranean culture. However, though it included several women writers such as Marita Bonner and Zora Neale Hurston, the Harlem Renaissance was a multifaceted movement emphasising the cultural revival of the African-American community as a whole, and did not focus on the gender issue. The civil rights movement in the 1950s, as discussed above, perpetuated sexism within the community. The negative image of the Black woman was further consolidated by mainstream media, and the stereotypes they generated further marginalised Black women.

This complete obliteration of the traces of their existence and the non-availability of a discursive space to articulate their realities and voice their experiences as women, led to Black women demanding a platform to assert their identity. African-American feminism or Black feminism has its roots in activism. It traces the historical existences and utterances of Black women who actively lived their lives, survived oppression within and outside their community and disappeared through the cracks of history. Black feminism aims at retrieving their narratives about themselves and their community. The community has an important role to play in Black feminism. It forms an integral part of the subjective self. An important work in this area is Alice Walker's *In Search of Our Mother's Gardens* (1983).

Walker engages in a study and analysis of the matrilineal traditions in Black feminism. In the preface to the book, she uses the term 'womanist' and writes that 'womanist is to feminist as purple to lavender', implying that Black feminism does not assume an oppositional stance to feminism but is nonetheless different from everything accepted as part of feminist discourses (Walker, *In Search of Our Mother's Gardens* ix). She adds that womanism is about the 'survival and wholeness of an entire people, male and female', dismissing the idea of gender as dealing with only one section of the human population and making it more inclusive and broader (ix).

In Search of Our Mother's Gardens puts forth the concept of alternative sources of history, such as creative and literary forms of expression, being used as sources to trace the traditions of continuity among Black women. Largely uneducated and denied all forms of documented expression, the individual utterances of Black women of the past seem to have been embedded in the community narratives of shared creativity, such as stories passed on orally from one generation to the next, quilts and gardens – the common forms of female creative activities. These forms of expression constitute alternative archives to mainstream historiography, documenting the lives of Black women as gendered subalterns – doubly marginalised and silenced by mainstream history.

In her poem titled 'Women', Walker ponders on

> How they knew what we
> Must know
> Without knowing a page
> Of it
> Themselves ('Women' 159)

emphasising the idea of the continuity of a tradition of articulation, and resistance begun by Black women of previous generations, whose foresight seems to have enabled the present generation of Black women to be where they are. Black feminism, therefore, advocates an exploration of alternative forms of expression to study the lives of Black women as subjects. This branch of feminism led to the emergence of a varied and rich tradition of literary representations through the works of Black women writers such as Gwendolyn Brooks, Zora Neale Hurston, Toni Morrison, Alice Walker and Maya Angelou, to name a few.

Postcolonial Feminism

Postcolonial feminism evolved in the late-twentieth century as an approach seeking to address the concerns of women in the postcolonial context – those concerns which were not covered by postcolonialism or mainstream European feminism. Since individual identity is a construct shaped and nurtured by multiple markers – such as caste, ethnicity, race and class – each individual derives a subject-position with reference to his/her history and culture, which is exclusive to him/her. Based primarily on this proposition, postcolonial feminism seeks to interrogate the universalist claims of mainstream European feminism regarding the rights and requirements of women in the Third World. It explores the fissures and ruptures in the subjecthood of postcolonial women created by their immediate cultural and historical positioning which in turn, constructs their individuality and defines their needs as distinctly different from those of European women.

A major contribution in this direction was made by Gayatri Chakravorty Spivak. In her essay 'Can the Subaltern Speak?' (1988), Spivak notes that the Third World woman is caught between tradition and modernisation, displacing her identity as a woman between subjecthood and objectification within this larger convoluted matrix of patriarchy and imperialism. To categorise the Third World woman in the same category as the Third World man takes away from the former as a subject, a major means of understanding her subject-position which is shaped and guided by specific patriarchal acculturation. The man, here, though belonging to the same class, is the oppressor, while the woman is doubly subjugated, in terms of class as well as gender.

Chandra Talpade Mohanty, in 'Under Western Eyes: Feminist Scholarship and Colonial Discourses' (1984), argues that gender and patriarchy cannot be conceptualised as universally applicable unidirectional power structures. They are culture-specific and hence heterogeneous, implying that manifestations of gender and patriarchy are different for diverse sections of women, according to their geo-temporal subject-positions. Third World women, she argues, are subjugated by multiple discourses of gender and patriarchy co-existing with other factors such as class and caste. They, therefore, cannot be represented or spoken for by mainstream European feminists, and their concerns and experiences cannot be voiced as part of the homogenised mainstream feminist discourse. The practice of representing the Third World woman as a silent subaltern is in itself a perpetuation of the colonial hegemonic discourse around feminism. In her *Feminism Without Borders: Decolonizing Theory, Practicing Solidarity* (2003), Mohanty explores the political, economic and social inequalities that coalesce in the subjugation of Third World women as they provide cheap labour as underpaid and unrecognised workers serving their immediate oppressors who dominate on grounds of class, race and gender. She calls for solidarity of women across the nations in order to attain equality and stability.

Trinh T. Minh-ha also explores the relationship between First World women and Third World women in her *Woman, Native, Other: Writing Postcoloniality and Feminism* (1989). She critiques the homogenisation based on gender which is imposed upon Third World women by First World feminists, and argues that such homogenisation obliterates the diversity of Third World contexts and experiences, and diminishes the identity of Third World women. In the process, First World women act as an extension of the patriarchal power structures which exclude and subordinate women in the Third World.

In the context of India, feminism as a perspective includes a plethora of other factors, besides gender – for instance, class, caste and location. These factors define the experiences of the women in India and demarcate the differences among them, thereby dismissing the idea of a homogenised category even within the cartographic boundaries of a single political unit called the nation. The urban women, for instance, do not identify with the causes and concerns of their rural counterparts. Belonging to areas that are less developed, the latter are subjected to a more intensive exploitation by several power structures which might exist as local units of administration; and these may not be applicable to the former. Further, patriarchal dominance is also likely to be more intense in the rural areas as a result of factors such as low female literacy and prevalence of child marriage. Similarly, women belonging to economically backward classes experience a completely different range of exploitation and dominance when compared to the women who belong to more affluent classes. The former are doubly marginalised on the grounds of their class as well as gender.

Apart from class, the component of caste is another important marker constituting the identity of the woman as the gendered subaltern. Caste and gender in the case of women belonging to subjugated castes do not form two mutually exclusive domains. Much like the African American feminist discourse, in this case, caste and gender operate as overlapping grounds of oppression, leading to double marginalisation of women. These women are oppressed at multiple levels – by the upper castes, by the men of their own caste, and by patriarchy in general. This realisation that women of the upper castes cannot comprehend or voice the experiences of women belonging to the oppressed castes, led Ruth Manorama to establish the National Federation of Dalit Women in 1995.

In his article titled 'Dalit Women Talk Differently' (1995), Gopal Guru explains how caste-identity becomes an important factor defining the experiences of Dalit women, and cites this as the reason why they refute 'the claim of upper caste women to dalithood'. He adds that they, therefore, consider 'the feminist theory developed by non-dalit women as unauthentic since it does not capture their reality' (2549). However, in a counter-discourse propounded in 'Dalit Women Talk Differently: A Critique of "Difference" and Towards a Dalit Feminist Standpoint Position' (1998), Sharmila Rege observes that this claim to exclusivity on the grounds of experience may 'limit the emancipator potential of the dalit women's organizations and also their epistemological standpoints' (WS 44). She calls for a merging of the Dalit and non-Dalit standpoints and concludes that though non-Dalit women may not be able to represent or speak for Dalit women, they can 'reinvent themselves as dalit feminists' (WS 45) by sharing Dalit subjectivities.

Feminist discourse in Subaltern Studies seeks to address and analyse the subject-position of these women who are doubly marginalised and suppressed by multiple power structures. It is an intersectional area of study where gender becomes the primary, but not the sole, cause of oppression. It coalesces with a close analysis of the other factors of oppression along with gender, such as race, class and caste. Subaltern feminism, hence, calls for the researcher to carefully investigate and disentangle the multiple threads of oppression which constitute the gendered subaltern as a subject.

THEORISING SUBALTERN FEMINISM

Soon after the formation of the Subaltern Studies group in India in the 1980s, Spivak wrote an interesting critique of the approach of the group using deconstructionist techniques, in her essay 'Subaltern Studies: Deconstructing Historiography' published in *Subaltern Studies, Volume IV* (1985). She observes that the Subaltern Studies Collective proposes a revision of the mainstream nationalist historiography on two lines: firstly, that 'the moments of change be pluralized and plotted as confrontations rather than transition'; and secondly, that 'such changes are signaled or marked by a functional change in sign-systems' (Guha 330). Interrogating not just the inclusions and exclusions of historiography, Spivak problematises the linguistic and narrative structures of historical discourse. She adds that when a theory of change enables interpretations by acting as a rupture between the sign and the meaning, it facilitates reading as an act of dynamic interaction between the past and the future.

In this sense, ascribing a subject-position to the subaltern in the seemingly linear discursive structure of history enables one to identify the cracks or fissures in the documented narrative, by lending to the event the possibility of an alternative interpretation and analysis. The subaltern is represented and re-presented in the process, and is thus ultimately *spoken for* by a sympathetic historiographer, rather than *speaking in his/her own right*. Spivak observes that the strategy of Subaltern Studies to claim a subject-position for the subaltern must be reinscribed in the context of the gendered subaltern. She exemplifies her point with reference to the role of rumours and women in her essay. While she refers to the former as the undocumented, oral but strategic mode of subaltern communication, the woman, she asserts, is an important 'concept-metaphor' who in conforming to the patrilineal and patrilocal trajectories of her life 'syntaxes patriarchal continuity even as she is herself drained of proper identity' (Guha 362).

According to Spivak, of the subaltern identified on the basis of class divisions in the context of colonised India, the woman, when studied separately as a representative of subalternity, emerges to be doubly subjugated. Her subaltern identity is defined not only by class in the larger nationalist domain of historiography, but also by gender within her own society and community. The identity of the woman as subaltern problematises a universal understanding of hegemony as being only colonial in its nature, for the patriarchal subjugation of the subject in question cannot be overlooked. Within the same structure of discursive analysis, thus, the woman as a subject of subalternity may be seen as subjected to more than a single power structure, unlike the man – she is doubly marginalised. It is here that the role of the historian and researcher representing the subaltern becomes important in introducing a counter-hegemonic discourse against the prevalent power hierarchies.

In *In Other Worlds* (1987), Spivak explores the gendered subaltern as a subject for history and literature. She observes that history is essentially a 'discursive narrativization of events' and adheres to a language which is 'structured or textured like what is called literature' (243). Hence, while engaging in an assessment of the subaltern subjectivity, the difference between history and literature is 'a difference in degree rather than in kind', because the subaltern status, being enshrouded in silence, is equally distant to both the disciplines and calls for a blending of reality and imagination in order to attain historical plausibility (243). She validates her point with reference to a translation of Mahasweta Devi's story titled *Stanadayini* ('Breast-Giver'). She argues that Jashoda – the protagonist of this story – could have existed as a subaltern in a specific historical moment as portrayed by Mahasweta Devi, and the assumptions made by the writer here in ascribing an identity to Jashoda are not very different from those of a subalternist historian who imagines a historical moment to retrieve the subaltern utterance.

Hence, in terms of race, class and caste, the identity of the gendered subaltern calls for a careful reimagining and analysis of the historical moment. This perspective widens not just the scope of Subaltern Studies but also the range of looking at the subaltern as a subject. It liberates the subject of subalternity from the restricted domains of history as the sole means of archival resource, to include alternative narratives available in other forms across literature and culture.

Another major representation of subalternity in the context of Third World women may be found in the writings of Dalit women. Dasari Kejiya and Sampathbabu Tokala, in their 'The Representations of Dalit Feminism Writings as Contention to Patriarchy' (2016), define Dalit literature as 'an attempt to articulate unheard, unspoken voices' (401). They constitute the subject-position obliterated by mainstream archives and documents. In *Writing Caste, Writing Gender* (2013), comprising autobiographies of eight Dalit women, Sharmila Rege argues that the autobiographies are not just narratives of pain and suffering. Referring to them as *testimonios*, Rege notes that these narratives do not intend to focus on literariness. Rather, they strive to communicate the realities of oppression and struggle faced by the subaltern groups. She adds that these narratives 'violate the parameters set by bourgeoisie autobiography and create testimonios of caste-based oppression, anti-class struggles and resistance' (14).

READING THE GENDERED SUBALTERN IN LITERARY REPRESENTATIONS

The existence of the gendered subaltern may be analysed through the literary representations documenting their lives. These representations span across the genres of fiction, poetry and autobiographies written by subaltern women or writers engaged in an attempt to recreate moments of social history to convey the stories of their lives. While stories are based on re-imagining geo-temporal contexts and have a definite conclusion, autobiographies portray the minute details of harsh realities endured as part of a perpetuated social practice. As discussed above, Spivak explores the role of literature in re-inscribing a subject-position to the gendered subaltern using Mahasweta Devi's stories, while Bama has provided a detailed record of social practices based on caste hierarchy in her autobiography *Karukku*. In *In Other Worlds* (1987), Spivak provides translations of two short stories by Mahasweta Devi – 'Draupadi' and 'Breast-Giver'. These stories attempt to trace the lives of two subaltern women who are marginalised and oppressed by several power hierarchies simultaneously. Dopdi Mejhen, the female protagonist of the first short story, is named so after the major mythological character Draupadi from the epic *Mahabharata*. However, in the story, Dopdi belongs to an aboriginal community engaged in a war of subsistence against the nation state, along with her husband Dulna Majhi, and she pronounces her name as 'Dopdi', implying a derivative as well as a deviation from the Sanskrit original. The power of the state is represented by Senanayak, the chief of the state's armed forces. Dulna and Dopdi use 'primitive weapons' and the 'baby scythe' in Dopdi's palm is the 'comfort of a half moon' (193). The story traces how Dulna is killed and Dopdi is captured by the forces led by Senanayak. Dopdi is eventually raped repeatedly by the men belonging to the armed forces including Senanayak, and the story ends with Dopdi walking naked towards Senanayak with 'her head high', as she says, 'You can strip me, but how can you clothe me again?' (196). The subjecthood of the victim of sexual violence that Dopdi becomes is particular to the subaltern woman in an otherwise gender-neutral context of resistance against oppression.

Spivak, in her analysis of the story, uses the technique of deconstruction to recognise the provisional and intractable starting points in the investigative endeavour, and to disclose the complicities so as to identify the opposition. Senanayak, who is given no first name or surname by the author, is known by his patronymic, suggesting a critique of man's self-adequate identity. Mahasweta Devi rewrites the epic episode of Draupadi in a different context and social scenario where she is stripped and insists on remaining publicly naked. The subversion of the mythological version occurs in the fact that there is no divine intervention to save Dopdi Mejhen's 'modesty'. It is here that the mythological Draupadi of

Aryan lineage differs from Devi's Dopdi belonging to an aboriginal community. This lack of divine intervention highlights the juncture where a male leadership ceases to protect and safeguard. Dopdi is what Draupadi was, but she also becomes what Draupadi could not be. The concept of shame associated with the woman's body is a bourgeoisie concept and valid only as long as it is affordable. When Dopdi crosses the sexual differential and utters her last words to Senanayak, she becomes a powerful subject, and Devi notes that 'for the first time Senanayak is afraid to stand before an unarmed target, terribly afraid' (Spivak 196). Spivak reads into this story 'an allegory of the woman's struggle within the revolution in a shifting historical moment' (184). She compares the Senanayak – who can theoretically identify with the enemy but in practice must destroy them – with the First World feminists and their self-congratulatory knowledge of the Third World.

In the second story, 'Breast-Giver', the protagonist is named Jashoda. Her name is spelt in line with the Bengali pronunciation of the name 'Yashoda', foster-mother to Krishna, the eighth avatar of Lord Vishnu, according to the Hindu legends. Yashoda is culturally recognised to be the archetype of motherly love and affection irrespective of biological ties. Jashoda, in the story, is a wet-nurse and the writer declares that she 'had taken motherhood as her profession', thereby subverting the socio-cultural myth of motherhood associated with the woman (Spivak 222). She is referred to as the 'Cow of Fulfillment' by the mistress of the Haldar household as Jashoda feeds the children and the women in the house can afford yearly pregnancies while 'keeping their figures' (227). However, with the death of the mistress and the new winds of change entering the women's quarters, the family splits up. The ageing Jashoda finds her worth diminished as the milk in her breasts dries up. Abandoned by her husband and sons, she is compelled to accept the position of a cook in the Haldar household and live with the other servants of the house. Jashoda is detected to be suffering from breast cancer and eventually dies a painful death all alone in a hospital. Her body lies unclaimed in the hospital morgue and she is finally cremated by an untouchable. The story ends with the author commenting that 'Jashoda's death was also the death of God' (240).

In turning fostering into a profession, Mahasweta Devi portrays mothering in its materiality, beyond its social and cultural implications. The life of Jashoda, as represented in the story, focuses upon the subaltern as a gendered subject – doubly oppressed by her class as well as gender. Jashoda provides sexual labour to her husband by bearing him several children, and also running his household by working as wet-nurse in the Haldar household. Yet, she is deserted by her husband as well as her children once she runs out of her prime. Her breast milk is her capital. The milk she produces for her children is through necessary labour while that she provides to the master's family is through surplus labour. To ensure the production of surplus in this case, the sexual division of labour is reversed. The emergence of value from Jashoda's labour-power infiltrates Marxism and interrogates its gender-specific assumptions by dismantling the labour theory of value which presupposes that the woman is subordinated within the class-society due to her dependence on the man who provides her with subsistence during the child-bearing period.

Mahasweta Devi interpreted *Stanadayini* as 'a parable of India after decolonization' where India as a nation is placed at the subject-position of Jashoda, the subaltern, providing nourishment to all classes and sections of people depending upon her. If she continues to be abused ruthlessly, she would also succumb to a self-consuming cancer. Jashoda voices the pathos of India as she lies alone in the hospital and hallucinates that every individual around her has been suckled by her. The doctor treating her comments, 'She sees her milk-sons all over the world' (Spivak 240). This plight of the nurturer interrogates the socio-cultural perspectives that deify motherhood while devaluing the mother. The comparison is made more pronounced by the continuous reference to the female deity worshipped as the 'lion-seated' in the story. According to Spivak, the cancer in Jashoda's body becomes 'the signifier of the oppression of the gendered subaltern' (267). It is caused by continuous abuse at multiple levels and concludes in the obliteration of the individual.

While Mahasweta Devi in her fiction focuses on the individual in history and strives to re-create the moment of the subaltern utterance, autobiography, as a literary genre, records first-person narratives of women who have been marginalised at multiple levels. While Dopdi and Jashoda are women subalternised by class and gender, caste oppression in subaltern feminism surfaces in the writings of Dalit women.

The publication of Bama's *Karukku*, originally in Tamil in 1992, was the inauguration of a new genre – a Dalit woman wrote her autobiography voicing the exploitation and patterns of subjugation which form an integral part of the social fabric in India and continue to be overlooked by the mainstream. In her preface to the second edition of *Karukku* in English translation, Bama writes 'that book was written as a means of healing my inward wounds' and recollects the varied responses that it received when it was first published (ix). The journey of her book took a new turn when it was translated into English by Lakshmi Holmström, and it soon earned international acclaim.

In *Karukku*, Bama focuses on caste-based oppression. It engages in an exploration of the double standards practised by representatives of institutional religion – in this case, Christianity – with reference to caste-based subjugation. Though, unlike her later work *Sangati* (1994), *Karukku* does not specifically highlight the plight of Dalit women, nonetheless, the role of women within the community and their lives of relentless labour within their homes and outside, is portrayed in *Karukku*. For instance, Bama notes that 'even if they did the same work, men received one wage, women another. They always paid men more' (*Karukku* 55). This highlights the accepted norms of devaluing the labour provided by women within the patriarchal structure of economy. In *Sangati*, which may be read as a kind of collective *testimonio* of women within the parayar community, and where Bama addresses the question of gender inequality more directly, she observes how the men could do whatever they liked with the money that they earned, while women were supposed to use their money for running their families.

Physical violence is presented as a normalised practice faced by the women of the parayar community. Referring to Uudan in *Karukku*, Bama recalls how 'he'd drag his wife by the hair to the community hall and beat her up as if she were an animal' (61). And yet, this would not draw any intervention from the other people within the community who 'came to watch' but could not 'go near and separate them' (61). The community also imposed restrictions upon the women's mobility and choices, such as ensuring that 'none of the women from our (Parayar) community went to the cinema' because they feared that if they did, 'the boys of all the other communities would pull our women' (58). This shows how Dalit women are doubly oppressed by patriarchy, where on the one hand they are abused by their own men, and on the other, they run the constant risk of being sexually violated by the men outside their community.

Yet, the service that the women render to their community is undeniable in the gender roles they play as mothers, wives and daughters. Even the girl children 'had to look after all the chores at home' (*Karukku* 52). Their role in ensuring the survival of the community is at par with that of the men. Bama recollects an intercaste conflict in her village and notes how when the men were chased by the police and had to seek refuge in the fields, hiding from the police, it was the women who would care for the children and make life go on in the village. She recalls the sexual vulnerability of these women as the policemen 'told them that since their husbands were away they should be ready to entertain the police at night, winked at them, and shoved their guns against their bodies' (40). Bama narrates how, during this time, when a small boy had died in the village and his father was hiding from the police, the women cleverly planned and arranged for the father to attend the child's funeral by making him 'wear a sari, disguise himself as a woman, cover his head, and pretend to be a mourner attending the funeral' (42). This instance provides an important insight into the social structure where the idea of a man dressing as a woman is considered as an assault on masculinity, irrespective of caste or community. In this context, it is the gendered manner of dressing, however, that seems to ensure the oppressors of unquestioned servitude and absolute harmlessness.

Sangati (1994) by Bama, on the other hand, focuses on the experiences of Dalit women within their community and is written in the form of anecdotes. Divided into twelve chapters, the stories and anecdotes in *Sangati* have different women characters as their narrators, and there is no fixed plot. At the very beginning, Bama states the purpose of writing *Sangati* and reveals that her 'mind is crowded with many anecdotes: stories not only about the sorrows and tears of dalit women, but also about their lively and rebellious culture, passion about life with vitality, truth, enjoyment and about their hard labour' (09). It is this aspect of the existence of Dalit women that *Sangati* explores and conveys to the reader. In addition to the representation of multiple layers of exploitation faced by Dalit women, it also records the coping strategies adopted by these women. One such strategy is their use of oral traditions in the form of folk lores, folk songs and rhymes which form a part of the culture that the women share amongst themselves, especially on special occasions and community events such as weddings. These forms of oral literature also serve as the source of their rootedness within the community and a means of asserting their culture. Another strategy of resistance adopted by these women is the use of abusive language. The enormous amount of physical labour which the women have to perform, besides satisfying the sexual requirements of their men, and the ill treatment that they receive at the hands of their own men as well as the larger society, leads them to use language as an instrument of their rebellion in order to vent their anger, fatigue and despair.

Autobiographies of Dalit women reveal situations which form an integral part of the lives of subaltern women, which remain absent from the mainstream archives. Another recent anthology relevant in this context is *Dalit Lekhika: Women's Writings from Bengal* (2020). Edited by Kalyani Thakur Charal and Sayantan Dasgupta, the collection consists of three sections – stories and poems by the current generation of Dalit women and an autobiographical section titled 'My Childhood' written by Kalyani Thakur Charal. In her Introduction to the volume, Charal observes that 'in Bengal, caste discrimination is concealed under the shroud of class discrimination', and relates how the major sociopolitical events in Bengal such as the Tebhaga Movement 'saw the involvement of very large numbers of Dalit and Adivasi women even though the leadership was in the hands of the upper classes' (Charal xiv). She refers to the politics of publication and states that there is 'no separate space for the Dalit women writers' who have been published in a 'rather desultory and haphazard manner' (Charal xvi). This anthology is unique in compiling the perspectives of several current women writers who are Dalit, and through their writings they put forth the disturbing realities which form a part of the experiences of Dalit women. Some of the stories in the volume also represent the progress made by Dalit women who despite their subjugated subject-positions seek to assume control over their own lives and sexuality. One such story is 'The Ghat of the Date Palm Tree and Panchi's Sense Organs' written by Saptadwipa Adhikari. Panchi Rishidas, the protagonist of the story, is a young girl around twelve years old, who lives with her parents and dreams of only 'sufficient quantity of rice – thrice, every day, all her life' (Charal 82). She attends the wedding of a cousin nine years older than her, and in a conversation between her newly married cousin, Hasi, and her friend, happens to overhear the two speaking of farming, bull and plough. Unaware that these were sexual innuendos being used by the two girls to discuss conjugal life, Panchi, who had always wanted to acquire a piece of land so that she could cultivate sufficient rice for herself and her family, determines to get married. The innuendos used in this context may be read from an ecofeminist perspective as they equate the woman with the land.

Panchi is married off to a physically challenged man, known as Langra Bishe for being lame. On the night of their wedding, Panchi is shocked as her husband uses the same innuendos used by Hasi to coerce her into submission and intercourse. Panchi refuses to satisfy his sexual cravings and returns to her parental house within a few days of the marriage. Marriage to her was just a means of acquiring a full meal. Having been denied that much, the patriarchal institution of marriage no longer holds any meaning for her. She begins working at other people's houses for food. It is only with her attainment of puberty that she understands the phallic association of the date palm tree and the agricultural metaphors used by her cousin Hasi. She declares to her mother, 'wives do not need husbands; it is the husbands who need wives', thereby revealing the contrast between the status of the woman in marriage as determined by patriarchal norms and the reality where men feed upon their wives like parasites (Charal 97). The story ends with Panchi determined to find a means of earning for herself so that she might be able to procure sufficient food for herself and her family. The pathos evoked by the story lies in the reader's acknowledgement of hunger being a major factor shaping the lives and realisations of people like Panchi. The story is also significant as it ends with Panchi acquiring uncompromised agency over her own life and body.

While the plight of Dalit women is represented in these stories, it is important to note that these stories are mostly written in regional languages and then translated into English. The reason behind this is the fact that Dalit women mostly use their native languages as the only available medium to record their experiences. The researcher/ scholar of subaltern feminism must therefore have access to the original texts and be versed with the nuances of the process of translation, because this is essentially an area of interdisciplinary investigation. The content is rooted in the prevalent social practices and norms. However, in the works of writers such as Meena Kandasamy, the content of expression related to caste-consciousness undergoes a huge change. Expressing herself in English and voicing the anguish of the gendered subaltern also oppressed on the basis of caste, Kandasamy radicalises her use of language to voice, and yet simultaneously transcend, the domains of caste-based oppression, and creates a world of her own where suffering is etched against a general narrative of pain.

In her poem 'Ekalaivan', based on the mythological figure of Ekalavya from the *Mahabharata,* Kandasamy recollects the tradition of exploitation established by the savarnas from the mythological times and foresees in this fable of injustice the seeds of a future insurgency. Ekalavya, in mythology, was a tribal prince with tremendous expertise in archery. He was self-taught but inspired by Guru Dronacharya who trained the Kauravas and the Pandavas. He made a statue of Dronacharya out of clay and considered it to be his teacher. When Dronacharya learnt about this, fearing that Ekalavya's skills might prove better than that of his own disciples, he asked Ekalavya for his right thumb as *gurudakshina*. In her poem, Kandasamy begins with a note of 'consolation' and writes, '... fascist Dronacharyas warrant / left-handed treatment' (99). Her use of the term 'fascist' represents her indignation towards an entire culture of caste-based exploitation. The poem ends with the reassurance that the Ekalavyas of the present will not need their right thumbs to fight caste oppression. It envisions an uprising of the oppressed against the oppressors, and justifies social uprising as an answer to the tradition of dominance and exploitation based on caste.

In another poem, 'Touch', Kandasamy addresses the trauma of an individual who has faced caste oppression. Beginning with a description of meditation – an act which calls for undivided concentration and '... keeping your mind as blank/ as a whitewashed wall ...' – Kandasamy refers to the sense of 'touch' as being the sole distraction in the process. The poem ends with an address to the reader and reminds them that 'touch', in the context of caste oppression, 'was a paraphernalia of / undeserving hate' (Web, n. p.). These lines crystallise much in their attempt to convey the humiliation faced by the caste-oppressed individual in multiple forms, at multiple levels. It is important to note Kandasamy's selection of 'meditation' as the context in this poem. Meditation or 'Yoga' in Hindu theology is considered as a means of achieving union with the Supreme Being. Its power is ascertained to be so much so that the eighteenth chapter of the Bhagavad Gita deals with the subject of Yoga and the various forms of Yoga. Here, the same is invoked by Kandasamy and entirely subverted as the awareness of 'touch' – a perception related to the skin – is seen to completely topple the state of mental calm and inner peace professed by the act of meditation.

In fact, many of Kandasamy's poems draw upon the Hindu theological doctrines as the dominant subtext. For instance, in 'Advaita: The Ultimate Question', she refers to the Vedanta doctrine of non-duality which proclaims that there is no other reality except the Brahman – a concept also stated in the *Brihadaranyaka Upanishad*. She leads the readers through a series of questions in the poem, finally culminating in the rhetorical question: Can an 'Untouchable Atman' and a 'Brahmin Atman' ever be equal? The crafting of her lines is such that the solitary interrogation mark in the last line questions the entire range of double standards established and practised as tradition in the name of institutional religion.

'Becoming a Brahmin' is another strikingly transgressive poem by Kandasamy. Described as an 'algorithm' to be used to transform a 'Shudra into a Brahmin', the poem prescribes six steps for a Savarna conversion. It begins with making an attractive Avarna girl get married to a brahmin. She must then bear him a daughter, who must then get married to a brahmin. These steps repeated six times will lead to 'the end product' which is 'a Brahmin'. In six lines, the poem voices the subject-position of the caste-oppressed woman, who is not only the caste-inferior but also the vessel who must be penetrated by the upper-caste in order to be able to ensure that her children might at some point of time, gain the status of the venerated upper-caste. It is also a scathing comment on the patriarchal assumption of the Hindu marriage which believes in the *gotraantar* of the woman after marriage – that is, once a woman is married, she becomes subsumed in the caste and clan of her husband.

While women's writings in Dalit literature and postcolonial feminism highlight the experience of exploitation at the levels of caste, class and gender, a parallel expression of multilayered dominance experienced by women on the basis of race and gender may be seen in the writings of African American women writers, such as Zora Neale Hurston, Toni Morrison and Alice Walker. In *Their Eyes Were Watching God* (1937), Hurston provides one such narrative of a woman named Janie Crawford. Written in the form of a retrospective narrative, the novel has Janie as a woman in her forties narrating the story of her life to her friend Pheoby. Her background presents a view of the hardships faced by African American women as it is revealed that her grandmother, Nanny, was a slave. Nanny was raped by her white owner, and gave birth to Janie's mother, Leafy. As Janie tells Pheoby about her journey through three marriages, she also narrates the story of an African American woman's journey towards self-determination. When she walks out of her first marriage, arranged by Nanny as a practical requirement, her rejection of her apron is symbolic of rejecting the gender role of essential servitude. Her second husband, Joe Starks, treats her as if she was his property, and his death liberates Janie, allowing her to live a life of freedom. As she later marries

Tea Cake, who is much younger to her, she exercises her choice. In the character of Tea Cake, Hurston provides a glimpse of the liberated African American identity. It is through her life with him that Janie acquires her sense of self and carves out her own identity. Written during the Harlem Renaissance, the narrative technique and the motifs used in *Their Eyes Were Watching God* closely follow folk traditions, especially the feature of replicability, because despite being the story of Janie, the narrative is designed to be repeated by many tellers within the community, at different points of time.

The community, in fact, forms an integral part of women's writing in Dalit literature, as also in African American literature. An important example of this may be found in *Beloved* (1987) by Toni Morrison. The novel is based around the death of the eldest child of Sethe. Sethe had killed her eldest daughter to save her from a life of slavery. The narrative in *Beloved* is based on memory and recollection. Beloved, as she emerges as a character in the novel, is the reincarnation of a painful past. The novel explores as its central theme the tension between the need to revive a forgotten past and the instinct to deny it. The ghost that haunts Sethe's house is an individual's consciousness of a collective past which the African American community has witnessed. In the process, Morrison rewrites history as memory. The point of view is that of a woman and the central theme relates to motherhood. Sethe kills Beloved as a response to the threat of a future of slavery – an apparent act of brutality that holds its meaning only against the larger context of the African American social history and the associated factors that could never be shaped by an individual. The reincarnation of Beloved is the resurrection of an anonymous victim from history, and Sethe's response to her presence is out of a sense of guilt. However, the act of murder and the feeling of guilt occur in two different time frames – each justified within its present context. Morrison, through the novel, suggests that the history of pain must be revived in order to be forgotten.

The Bluest Eye (1970), one of Morrison's earlier novels, also provides a glimpse of community life through the story of a young African American girl named Pecola Breedlove. Pecola is considered to be ugly by others, and dreams of having blue eyes one day. Inspired by the Caucasian ideals of beauty, she prays for blue eyes each night. For her, the colour blue is a source of identification with the Other and a simultaneous source of alienation from the Self. Twice raped by her father Cholly and abandoned by her mother Pauline, Pecola lives with her foster parents, the MacTeers, while expecting Cholly's child. Cholly is also revealed to have been a slave in the past – abandoned by his parents and tormented by white men, so much so that he ends up becoming a violent husband and an abusive father. Pauline, Pecola's mother, escapes from her miserable life as the housekeeper of a rich white family, while Sam, Pecola's brother, reacts to the immediate circumstances in his family by running away. Pecola inherits the burden of a painful collective history. She embodies the identity of the African American woman as the Other of the Other. The self-hatred of the Breedlove family is the most destructive element in their lives. The poignancy of Pecola's victimisation arises not only from gender and racism, but also from the intra-racial conflicts related to colour – firmly rooted in white racist myths and subscribed to by the African American culture. Pecola's foster sister Claudia – who detests the Caucasian dolls and desires to destroy them – emerges as a promise of a better tomorrow based on self-determination where the African American community will be able to dismiss the concept of the ideal as imposed by white people and rejoice in the celebration of their difference.

This difference and a sense of integrity with the African lineage finds a more explicit expression in *The Color Purple* (1982) by Alice Walker. The novel narrates, in an epistolary mode, the story of the protagonist Celie, against the backdrop of Georgia in the 1930s. Celie, who is abused and raped by her stepfather Alphonso and bears him two children, is married off to Albert who also physically, sexually and psychologically torments her. She has a sister named Nettie. The novel is written in the form of Celie's letters to God and sometimes to Nettie. It explores the strength of female friendships through the relationship shared by Celie and Sofia, the wife of Albert's son Harpo, and the bond shared by Celie and Shug, Albert's mistress. These friendships that the women share enable them to evolve as individuals in their personal spheres of existence –

they complement and complete each other. The voiceless subaltern, Celie, finds expression in her letters which are written in a confiding tone and reveal her psychological development. Walker uses strong motifs to highlight the African American identity, one of them being the act of quilting. Celie and Sofia decide to make a quilt together, out of messed-up curtains; Shug donates her old yellow dress for Celie's quilt; and Nettie uses the quilt made by Corrine to remind her of her meeting with Celie at the store. Thus, quilting becomes a shared exercise and the quilt becomes the expression of a shared past – social, cultural and political. The roots of a community existence are traced from Harlem to the shores of Africa through the life of Nettie who moves from Georgia to Africa through Harlem and returns to Georgia at the end of the novel. In one of her letters from Harlem, Nettie writes to Celie, 'We are not white. We are not Europeans. We are black like the Africans themselves' (122). This marks an instance of celebration of Black identity with a distinct allusion to the Harlem Renaissance and the rise of the New Negro.

The community, therefore, forms an important part of the writings of the gendered subaltern, across space and time. The collective unit of the community is the marker of individual identity in such works. The women who are subjected to various forms of exploitation within and outside their respective communities, nonetheless, derive their sense of identity from a shared existence with the other women in their community. This sharing might be material or emotional, or both. Their sense of individual self is not based on disintegration from the social and cultural roots. Their voices reflect traditional inheritances which are then appropriated to individual contexts and purposes. The characters – whether it is a Jashoda or a Celie – re-create the possibility of retrieving the lost utterance of a gendered subaltern whose existence is plausible within the historical frames of time, both past and present.

★★★

Postcolonial feminism, from the perspective of Subaltern Studies, opens up for the researcher/scholar new areas inviting exploration. While first-hand documentation of experiences provides a rich source of information, most of these documents written in native languages need to be translated in order to gain the attention of a larger readership. The literary representations, such as the ones discussed in this chapter, serve to portray the imagined lives – as opposed to the imaginary lives – of women within these spaces whose articulations are lost through the cracks and fissures of history. The chief characteristic of the nature of the expression of subaltern women is the hybridity of forms that it might assume – from the realms of accepted aesthetic modes of representation such as literary representations, to more indigenous and community-bound forms including everyday art.

For instance, in case of subaltern feminism, narratives might also take the form of alternative expressions – for instance, quilting, needlework or objects and experiences related to food or cooking such as moulds used for making sweets. It is important for the researcher to recognise and respond to these alternative forms of expression as first-hand documents because subaltern women mostly do not have access to formal education or aesthetic domains of literary expressions. An example of this may be found in the context of Bengal, where it was a common practice for women to prepare moulds meant for making sweets. Women whose lives were confined to their home and the kitchen would engrave brief messages or even riddles on these moulds, to be later deciphered by the women of the next generation. In another instance, narratives of life or certain episodes of life were preserved by women in the form of *naksikantha* or needlework on quilts and sarees so that their stories are preserved through generations. As noted by Spivak, the women as 'concept metaphors', by virtue of their patrilineal and patrilocal existence, used this form of communication as exclusive to their own kind which would escape patriarchal censorship and be passed on to the next generation as a flow of family traditions.

REFERENCES

Bama. *Karukku*. Tr. Lakshmi Holmström. Oxford UP, 2012.
----. *Sangati*. Tr. Lakshmi Holmström. Oxford UP, 2005.
Charal, Kalyani Thakur, and Sayantan Dasgupta, ed. *Dalit Lekhika: Women's Writings from Bengal*. STREE, 2020.

Guha, Ranajit, ed. *Subaltern Studies IV: Writings on South Asian History and Society*. Oxford UP, 1985.

Guru, Gopal. 'Dalit Women Talk Differently'. *Economic and Political Weekly* 30.41/42 (1995): 2548–50. JSTOR, <www.jstor.org/stable/4403327>.

hooks, bell. *Ain't I a Woman?* Pluto Press, 1982.

Hurston, Zora Neale. *Their Eyes Were Watching God*. Virago Press, 1986.

Kandasamy, Meena. 'Ekalavyan'. *Indian Literature* 50.4 (234) (2006): 99. JSTOR. <www.jstor.org/stable/23346415>.

----. 'Touch'. Poem Hunter. <https://www.poemhunter.com/poem/touch-65/>.

----. 'Advaita: The Ultimate Question'. Poem Hunter. <https://www.poemhunter.com/poem/advaita-the-ultimate-question/>.

----. 'Becoming A Brahmin'. Poem Hunter. <https://www.poemhunter.com/poem/becoming-a-brahmin/>.

Kejiya, Dasari, and Sampathbabu Tokala. 'The Representations of Dalit Feminism Writings as Contention to Patriarchy'. *International Journal of English Language, Literature and Translation Studies* (2016). <http://www.ijelr.in/3.1.16B/397--408%20Dr.%20DASARI%20KEJIYA.pdf.>

Minh-ha, Trinh T. *Woman, Native, Other: Writing Postcoloniality and Feminism*. Indiana UP, 1989. JSTOR, <http://www.jstor.org/stable/j.ctt16xwccc>.

Mohanty, Chandra Talpade. 'Under Western Eyes: Feminist Scholarship and Colonial Discourses'. *Boundary 2*.12/13 (1984): 333–58. JSTOR, <https://doi.org/10.2307/302821>.

----. *Feminism Without Borders: Decolonising Theory, Practicing Solidarity*. Zubaan Books, 2003.

Morrison, Toni. *The Bluest Eye*. Vintage. 1999.

----. *Beloved*. Vintage, 1999.

Mukhopadhyay, Arpita. *Feminisms*. Orient BlackSwan, 2016.

Rege, Sharmila. 'Dalit Women Talk Differently: A Critique of "Difference" and Towards a Dalit Feminist Standpoint Position'. *Economic and Political Weekly* 33.44 (1998): WS 39–WS 46. JSTOR, <www.jstor.org/stable/4407323>.

----. *Writing Caste, Writing Gender*. Zubaan Books, 2013.

Spivak, Gayatri Chakravorty. 'Can the Subaltern Speak?'. *Literary Theory: An Introductory Reader*. Ed. Saugata Bhaduri and Simi Malhotra. Anthem Press, 2010.
----. *In Other Worlds*. Routledge, 1988.
Walker, Alice. *In Search of Our Mother's Gardens*. Orion Books, 2011.
----. *The Color Purple*. Orient House, 2005.
----. 'Women'. *Alice Walker: Collected Poems*. Harcourt Brace Jovanovich, 2008. 159.

Chapter Five

Subaltern Studies and the Dalit Experience

Apart from class and gender, caste is another major criterion for identifying subalternity in the Indian context. The twelfth volume of *Subaltern Studies* (2005) focuses on caste and religion as markers of subalternity, and is titled *Muslims, Dalits and the Fabrications of History*. Caste, in the Indian social fabric, operates at two levels – as a unit of classification and as a system. As a unit of classification, caste has been operational in the Indian society and serving the purpose of social stratification, since the brahminical era. It is the function of caste as a system which leads to formation of hierarchies of oppression. However, the nature of this functionality has undergone several changes through different social orders and rules. The only constant factor has been the perpetuation of the cycle of victimisation.

Caste-based differences and prejudices have, since ages, constituted rigid demarcations of social existence in India. However, the idea of transcending the casteist hierarchy has been a part of the country's counter-traditions from the times of the Bhakti movement dating back to roughly the twelfth century. One may refer to the works of poet–saints such as Chokhamela (c. fourteenth century), Kabir (c. fifteenth century), Eknath (c. sixteenth century) and Dadu Dayal (c. sixteenth century) whose songs and poems represent attempts to interrogate the concepts of 'high' and 'low' in terms of religious sanctity, while preaching faith in the *nirguna*, or the formless God.

However, the exploration of the Dalit experience as an utterance and record of exploitation distinctively directed towards a particular section of the population on grounds of caste, has been a comparatively recent phenomenon. It may be dated from the works and writings of Jyotirao and Savitribai Phule in the nineteenth century. Within the geopolitical expanse of India, each community, each region and each ethnicity has its own experiences of caste and caste-based discriminations, ranging from oppression and ostracisation to a complete obliteration of social identity. Nonetheless, what is integral to the study of caste-based oppression is its intersectionality with class. Social stigma and prejudice invariably lead to an economically underprivileged position for a large section of the caste-oppressed population. This chapter shall explore caste as a marker of subalternity and the connections between the Dalit experience and Subaltern Studies.

SOCIAL AND HISTORICAL BACKGROUND

Caste as a system has served the purpose of stratification since the Vedic times. The idea of caste can be divided into two concepts – the concept of *varna* and the concept of *jaati*. *Varna* refers to the division of society into four groups comprising the brahmins, the kshatriyas, the vaishyas and the shudras. *Jaati*, implying birth, operates as a category within the fold of *varna* and branches out into several subdivisions. 'Caste' as a term was devised for administrative purposes and implies both *varna* and *jaati*. Initially meant to classify society in terms of occupations and an individual's obligations towards his/her community in the Vedic ages, caste divisions were later infused with rules of hierarchy by *Manusmriti*, an ancient *dharmashastra*. *Manusmriti* advocated evaluation of the worth of individuals depending upon their caste and encouraged control and subjugation of people belonging to the 'lower' castes by those of the 'higher' castes, thereby generating a concept of caste hierarchy which determines caste norms even today.

The term 'caste' is derived from the Portuguese term *casta* implying race, lineage or tribe, and was first used by the Portuguese to refer to the heterogeneous groups that formed the Indian society in the middle of the fifteenth century. The colonial administration appropriated the caste system as a method of social stratification to ensure administrative convenience. Of the many ethnographic studies conducted by the British administration, *The People of India* (1868–75), published in eight volumes by John Watson and John Kaye, remains significant. Containing annotated photographs of the people of different native castes and tribes of India, it was meant to document the people of India for ease of classification and administration, on the basis of physical attributes, traditions of clothing and other aspects of life. In 1908, Herbert Risley published another book with the same title. In addition to providing an ethnographic survey of the people of India, Risley's book acknowledged caste to be the primary functional unit which held together the diverse population of India within a standardised structural hierarchy.

G. S. Ghurye in his *Caste and Race in India* (1932) provided a comprehensive sociological perspective on the caste system. Beginning with a detailed survey of the features of the caste system, Ghurye observes that the British 'decided to leave the peculiar institutions of the country severely alone' except when they interfered with governance and maintenance of law and order (270). He traces the emergence of Indian cities of mixed populations in terms of caste, by arguing that the growth of industrial cities resulted in the migration of people from the fixed caste orders of their villages and communities. Oliver Cox, in *Caste, Class and Race* (1948), differentiated between the concepts of caste, class and race, and stated that as opposed to the concept of race, in the Hindu caste system, the members are 'attached to their caste' (Johnson 456). Hence, caste identity, according to Cox, unlike race or class, is not imposed by external factors but attained through birth and forms a social order of utmost complexity.

In *Homo Hierarchicus: The Caste System and Its Implications* (1966), a treatise on the Indian caste system, Louis Dumont examined caste as a key component defining the social structure of India and explored the functionality of caste as a determinant in terms of hierarchy and occupation. He also provided a detailed analysis of the manner in which caste as a system has its own laws related to contact and food, as well as marriage where caste identity is retained through the practice of endogamy. Of the Western conception of the Indian caste system, Dumont writes about three phases – the first is a period of explanation and documentation because it was a 'surprising or shocking' system to reckon with; the second is a period comprising descriptions; and the third, starting from 1945, is a period of intensive studies by anthropologists (Dumont 22).

M. N. Srinivas is credited with coining the term 'Sanskritisation' in order to explain caste mobility. In his *Caste in Modern India and Other Essays* (1962), Srinivas approaches the system as a social order from methodological, polemical as well as analytical perspectives. He uses the term Sanskritisation to refer to the propensity of the lower castes to adopt the practices of the upper castes in order to raise their social status. This process of Sanskritisation, in turn, led to the acceptance of the hegemonic discourses of brahminical orders, such as those propagated by the *Manusmriti*, as social norms.

Social segregation based on caste identity resulted in different forms and degrees of exploitation, including the formation of strict divisions and strictures related to occupation and livelihood. Even today, it is not unusual to come across caste names being used as derogatory terms, or suggestions that certain groups (castes) are inherently inferior in terms of competence or intelligence. Another instance is the glorification of the adolescent male child in brahmin families as an ordained brahmin, in the form of 'thread ceremonies' thoughtlessly performed as family or social gatherings. These perpetuate the caste order.

POLITICAL AND CULTURAL CONSCIOUSNESS OF CASTE: A HISTORY OF AWAKENING

In the nineteenth century, the renowned social activist Jyotirao Phule (1827–90) raised his voice against caste-based oppression and initiated efforts to educate lower-caste women of Maharashtra. He started India's first girls' school in 1848 at Bhide Wada in Pune. Phule himself was from a lower-caste family and had experienced humiliation based on his caste. He was assisted in his endeavours by his wife Savitribai Phule (1831–97). Having acquired education after marriage, Savitribai enrolled for two teacher training programmes, and was actively engaged in fighting oppression based on caste and gender. In 1873, Jyotirao Phule formed the Satyashodhak Samaj to work for the benefit of the oppressed castes and women (who were doubly subjugated – in terms of caste as well as gender). He is often credited with the coining of the term 'Dalit' to imply 'the oppressed'.

Phule's play *Gulamgiri* (1871) was written to glorify the English for raising their voice against slavery and advocating universal human rights. Written in the form of a dialogue between Jyotirao and Dhondirao, the play is a sharp critique of the *Manusamhita* as the origin of the caste system. *Gulamgiri* rebukes the entire Hindu pantheon and the stories of creation which justify a social hierarchy based on caste. It credits the English and Christians as people who acknowledge other human beings as equals and bestow upon all the basic human rights (especially with reference to the abolition of slavery). Though it may not be accurate in its assessment of the Western outlook, *Gulamgiri* continues to be one of the early revolutionary texts in the nineteenth century to voice the maladies of the caste system.

In the twentieth century, caste as a component of individual identity continued to divide large sections of the population comprising the lower castes as untouchables or those identified as *acchyut*. Ignominious customs continued to be practised as part of day-to-day social life in the name of caste norms and caste hierarchy. Towards the beginning of the century, Periyar E. V. Ramasamy (1879–1973) fought against caste oppression in Tamil Nadu and actively participated in the Vaikom Satyagraha (1924–25) directed against untouchability and caste discrimination. A member of the Indian National Congress from 1919 to 1925, Periyar was a proponent of anti-brahminism which shunned the idea of caste hierarchy and practices projecting the brahmin at the top of the caste hierarchy. In 1925, he joined the Self-Respect Movement which was founded on the principle that one who acquires self-respect cannot be deceived by the propaganda of exploitation. The movement remains popular in Tamil Nadu.

Mahatma Gandhi is credited with coining the term 'Harijans' to refer to the caste-oppressed community. He voiced the need for equality through the formation of All India Harijans Sevak Sangh in 1932. Though initially Gandhi used the term '*antyaja*', meaning the 'last-born', while campaigning against untouchability in the 1920s, he began using the term 'Harijan' in 1933, to imply the 'children of God'. In adopting this term, Gandhi was inspired by the medieval saint–poet Narsinh Mehta. However, though initially interpreted as a eulogistic coinage, the term was later rejected by people belonging to lower-caste communities as condescending, patronising and hypocritical.

Babasaheb Bhimrao Ambedkar (1891–1956), a pioneer who himself was from an oppressed caste, is associated with the political consciousness of caste, and led the Mahad Satyagraha in 1927. He dedicated his book *Who were the Shudras?* (1946) to Mahatma Phule, and called him 'the Greatest Shudra of Modern India'. Interrogating the *varna* system, Ambedkar's book traces the Vedic origins of the social practice. It subverts the familiar narrative of caste distinctions to assert that the shudras did not form a separate 'fourth' *varna* in the Indo-Aryan society, and that they were a part of the kshatriya *varna*.

Who were the Shudras? further states that there was a continuous feud between brahmins and shudra kings, which led the former to developing enmity towards the latter and stop performing any rituals or rites – including the *upanayana* – for them. Ambedkar argued that this led to the degradation of shudras' social status, and the perpetuation of this stabilised the social order. A significant role was also played by the Criminal Tribes Act of 1871, passed by the British government. The Act stated that if the local government 'believed that any tribe, gang or class of persons' is continually in the habit of committing non-bailable offences, then it could declare 'such tribe, gang or class to be a criminal tribe'. This political sanction for discrimination further justified the social division and stigma attached to certain sections of the population.

Discussing the role of caste as a marker of individual identity, Ambedkar observes, in *Annihilation of Caste* (1936), that 'the Hindu Society does not exist. It is only a collection of castes' (Ambedkar, *Annihilation of Caste*). In *The Untouchables* (1948), Ambedkar used the term 'broken men' to identify Dalits. However, Ambedkar himself used the colonial administrative term 'Depressed Castes', and later, following the setting up of a 'schedule' by the colonial government to provide reservations for untouchable castes, he started using the term 'Scheduled Castes'. It is the latter term which, consequently, appears in the Constitution of India which came into effect after the Independence.

The Constitution of India, as a political document, ensures for all the citizens certain forms of freedom under the Fundamental Rights. Right to equality, irrespective of caste, race, religion or sex is guaranteed in Articles 14–16. Any form of discrimination on the basis of race, caste, religion or sex is strictly prohibited, while Article 17 mentions that '"Untouchability" is abolished and its practice in any form is forbidden'. In matters of employment opportunities and prohibition of discrimination, Articles 15 and 16 add that the state can make special provisions to ensure the advancement of the Schedules Castes and the Scheduled Tribes. Further, Article 46 of the Directive Principles of State Policy prescribes, 'The State shall promote with special care the educational and economic interests of the weaker sections of the people, and, in particular, of the Scheduled Castes and the Scheduled Tribes, and shall protect them from social injustice and all forms of exploitation'.

However, political mobilisation never sanctions social consent to a counter-hegemonic proposal, and, hence, eradicating differences and exploitation in practice continues to be a difficult task. As David Ludden writes in his introduction to *Reading Subaltern Studies*, 'high-caste elites had always needed coercive power to keep low castes, peasants, workers and tribal groups in place' (9). The Dalit consciousness, therefore, remained largely unaddressed by mainstream historical documentation and constitutional policies aiming at public welfare and development.

The history of Dalit movements in India is varied. It is a study of subjugation, protests and at times, religious conversion (through choice or compulsion). There is no unified history of Dalit movements. The historical specificity of Dalit uprisings varies according to their location. For instance, the Dalit experience in Bihar or Uttar Pradesh is very different from that in Maharashtra or Andhra Pradesh. Similarly, Dalit utterances and expressions vary across regions. Also, it is often impossible to date these movements and utterances or document them using a general timeline. Hence, every study in this domain requires a careful balancing of history, and sensitivity on the part of the author as well as the researcher.

The word 'Dalit', first used by Mahatma Phule in the nineteenth century, was revived in the 1970s with the Dalit Panthers Movement which initiated a new cultural nationalism of the Dalit community. Inspired by the African American Black Panther Movement in its assertion of identity, the Dalit Panther Movement mobilised an entire section of people to come out in protest against the social oppression based on caste. This was occasioned by caste oppression which continued even after the Independence, through the 1950s, which forbade the lower castes from using public wells and tanks, entering temples, attending schools with 'Caste Hindus' or seeking dignified employment. The Dalit Panthers were established in 1972 in Bombay as a response to this sustained system of caste oppression.

V. T. Rajshekar published the first issue of the *Dalit Voice* – the first major English journal recording Dalit utterances – in 1981. In *Dalit: The Black Untouchables of India* (1987), Rajshekar drew a parallel between the liberation struggle of the African Americans and that of Dalits in India, interpreting the latter as an extension of the former. In fact, Janardhan Waghmare traces similarities between 'Black Literature and Dalit Literature' in his eponymous essay, stating that, primarily, 'both Black and Dalit writers are in search of their respective identities' (Dangle 321). Apart from establishing the term 'Dalit' as a signifier of protest and aspirations, the Dalit Panthers Movement brought together playwrights, poets and writers as representatives of the Dalit community, who claimed space for an alternative expression of subjectivity and culture in their works. It marked the beginning of a Dalit cultural nationalism and had a lasting impact on literature.

While, the early–twentieth-century literatures in the vernacular record scattered representations of the Dalit voice, an attempt to formalise these alternative expressions as a separate stream may be seen towards the end of the 1960s as Marathi writers like Baburao Bagul, Anna Bhau Sathe, Namdeo Dhasal, Arjun Dangle and

Yogiraj Waghmare came together to represent a distinct counterpoint to traditionalist mainstream upper-caste literatures. The Dalit Panthers Movement of the 1970s thus had a significant contribution in marking the beginnings of an organised and channelised stream of Dalit literature. The formation of the Dalit Panthers, politically, marked an important phase in the organisation of the caste-oppressed to claim their political and social rights. It marked the awakening of political demands and claims to civil rights. The 1980s saw the emergence of several political parties to voice the demands of Dalits. In 1982, the Dalit Panthers Iyakkam was formed in Madurai, Tamil Nadu, and a couple of years later, the Bahujan Samaj Party (BSP) was formed by Kanshi Ram on the birth anniversary of Bhimrao Ambedkar. With the formation of the BSP in 1984, the term 'bahujan', implying 'many' or 'majority' gained political currency to represent the caste-oppressed section of the population. The use of the term asserts the fact that the majority of the Indian population belongs to the lower castes and is hence subjugated. This term includes the Scheduled Castes, Scheduled Tribes and the Other Backward Classes (OBC) and does not imply only Dalits. Kancha Ilaiah Shepherd, in *Why I am Not a Hindu: A Sudra Critique of Hindutva Philosophy, Culture and Political Economy* (1996), traces the evolution of the terms associated with the caste-oppressed sections of the Indian society and uses the concept of 'Dalitbahujan' to refer to the 'people and castes who form the exploited and suppressed majority' (Ilaiah ix).

In terms of cultural revival and assertion of identity, the Bahujan Samaj Party played an important role by lending its support to the Dalit intellectuals who explored and documented oral histories related to the Uprising of 1857, and sought to rediscover the subaltern heroes of the rebellion belonging to lower castes as cultural icons representing the oppressed masses. In the process, a counter-discourse to the mainstream nationalist historiography emerged. The latter had acknowledged only the contribution of the aristocratic and ruling classes through figures such as Tantia Tope, Rani Lakshmibai and Begum Hazrat Mahal, in the narratives of the rebellion. The emerging Dalit consciousness placed against these known figures, their caste representatives such as Bhau Bakshi,

Puran Kori, Jhalkaribai, Uda Devi and Avantibai. In fact, this emerging Dalit consciousness claimed that the Uprising of 1857 was not initiated by Mangal Pandey, but by Matadin Bhangi, a worker from an untouchable community who asked Mangal Pandey for a mug of water, and in retaliation to the humiliation he was subjected to for his caste-identity, informed Pandey about the truth of the cartridges smeared with pig and cow fat. It is Bhangi, therefore, who has to be credited with arousing the soldiers' political consciousness, which then led to the insurgence. In his article 'Reactivating the Past: Dalits and Memories of 1857', Badri Narayan Tiwari notes that this process of rediscovering the role of the subaltern from oral traditions and popular songs known to the common people of Uttar Pradesh 'enabled the dalits to invent their heroes and histories who could become both local heroes and identity markers for the entire community in its everyday struggle for dignity and self-respect'. Similarly, in Bihar, the figure of the folk hero Chuharmal became the representative of the dusadh and bhangi communities against the upper-caste bhumiyars. In *Documenting Dissent: Contesting Fables, Contesting Memories and Dalit Political Discourse* (2001), Badri Narayan Tiwari shows how the theme of a street play called *Rani Reshma Chuharmal ka khela* which depicts Reshma, daughter of a bhumiyar, falling in love with Chuharmal, the righteous hero of the dusadhs, becomes the site of conflict for the two castes as they aim to appropriate this popular legend to serve their own cause.

Thus, the newly emergent political consciousness led to a simultaneous cultural awakening and assertion of Dalit (and other oppressed castes') identities. The fissures in historical narratives yielded spaces for the discovery and rise of subaltern identities representing communities of oppressed castes, and were gradually assimilated into the larger narrative of nationalist history as a counter-discourse voicing people's history (as opposed to the dominant elitist historiography) since the 1980s. The Mandal Commission, formed during the government led by Morarji Desai in 1979, identified 52 per cent of the Indian population as falling under the Other Backward Classes (OBC) category, who have suffered oppression on the grounds of caste and class. It suggested 27 per cent reservation for OBC job applicants in organisations under the central government and in public sector undertakings. The Commission's recommendations were implemented in 1992 during the regime of V. P. Singh. We have witnessed a gradual expansion of academic and ideological frameworks to assimilate subaltern perspectives of nationalist historiography. In an encouraging instance, a commemorative postage stamp in honour of Jhalkaribai was issued by the Indian Postal Department in 2001.

SUBALTERN STUDIES AND THEORISING DALIT CONSCIOUSNESS

Dalit literature offers an area of intersectional interpretation for Subaltern Studies researchers. As in the case of the Third World woman representing the doubly subjugated subaltern, the Dalit as a subject of Subaltern Studies also represents an individual at the receiving end of multiple layers of subjugation. Identity being a plural concept with changing manifestations in accordance with time and space, the Dalit as a subject, is oppressed on the grounds of nation, class, caste and, in the case of Dalit women, gender. Tracing the existence and voicing the subject position of the individual in this case, therefore, demands alternative archives of documentation, such as literary representations, written as well as oral, in the form of local/regional legends, autobiographies and cultural markers such as traditional artefacts.

In 'Dalit Movement in Mainstream Sociology', Gopal Guru provides a critique of the dominant theoretical approaches based on liberalism and the ideas of relative deprivation and social mobility used for analysing the Dalit experience. He argues that these approaches, distant from the Dalit subjectivity and experience, obstruct the development of a 'homogeneous Dalit consciousness' and lead the oppressed groups 'to organise their thought and action not on their own authentic terms but in the terms of those privileged sections whose hegemonic worldview underlies the structures of domination' (572). This argument is further explored in the book *The Cracked Mirror: An Indian Debate on Experience and Theory* (2012) by Gopal Guru and Sundar Sarukkai. The writers explore the distorted relation between experience and theory in the field of social sciences as far as Dalit studies are concerned, through the subterranean reality of the 'cracked mirror'. They emphasise experience as an essential component to the formulation of theory so as to facilitate a merging of the empirical and the conceptual. Articulation and subsequent theorisation based on experience is hence accorded more credibility as it posits experience (as opposed to imagination) as a category. This articulation of experience, however, does not remain uniform even within the Dalit caste identity. In another article, 'Dalit Women Talk Differently', Gopal Guru argues that the language of articulation of experience for Dalit women differs radically from those of other groups – non-Dalit feminist groups on the one hand and Dalit men, on the other. He says that the subjugation on the basis of gender does not consider the category of caste exploitation when voiced by non-Dalit, urban feminists; and within the caste-identity, the cultural domain is dominated by Dalit men who do not treat the literary output of Dalit women with seriousness.

Adding to this, Sharmila Rege observes that 'it is imperative for feminist politics that "difference" be historically located in the real struggles of marginalised women' (WS 39). She suggests that though experience, as stated by Gopal Guru, is essential to the articulation of the difference embedded in the narratives of Dalit women, to hold it as a compulsory component of Dalit feminism would further isolate Dalit women from other feminist groups on the basis identitarian segregation. Rege advocates a merging of the Dalit and non-Dalit feminist perspectives as collective identities, so as to effectively interrogate dominant patriarchal structures.

Similarly, the selection of a language for recording Dalit experiences has been negotiated from various angles. There are diverse standpoints regarding the use of English as the medium of expression for Dalit literature. Many argue that caste being a concept alien to its origin, English as a language does not contain the semiotic register to convey the nuances of the caste order. The languages used by Dalit writers themselves – such as Marathi by Sharankumar Limbale or Tamil by Bama – express the subtleties and shades of caste oppression with an ease and spontaneity that is unknown to their English translations.

Rita Kothari has noted that English as a language of expression provides the Dalit writer a 'wider dissemination' of their works and holds for them the promise of 'agency, articulation, recognition and justice' (60). Referring to Neerav Patel's article titled *Gujarati maari matrubhasha, English maari foster mother*, Kothari shows how Patel argues in favour of using English since it assures him of an escape from the dominant literary structures imposed by Gujarati which is dictated by the caste order. At the other end of the spectrum, she refers to young writers like Meena Kandasamy who write in English, and prefer the internet and cyber technology as mediums for disseminating their thoughts to a larger audience worldwide.

There are also debates regarding the aesthetic evaluation of literary works by Dalit writers, addressed by Sharankumar Limbale's *Towards an Aesthetic of Dalit Literature* (2004), and the extent of emphasis that should be laid on the caste identity of a Dalit writer as asked by Imayam, which are discussed later in the chapter. The researcher working on Dalit experience as a form of subalternity needs to recognise and disentangle this plurality of discursive standpoints while engaging with Dalit literature.

DALIT LITERATURE

The term 'Dalit literature' implies a corpus of literary works documenting the experiences of exploitation faced by the people belonging to Dalit communities. Though there are instances of literary works documenting Dalit experiences written by non-Dalit writers, such as *Untouchable* (1935) by Mulk Raj Anand, the idea of Dalit subjectivity in works identified as Dalit literature demands documentation and representation of subjugation by writers within the Dalit community. It emphasises speaking for oneself. The point of view in these works is that of an insider familiar with the patterns and practices of caste exploitation.

The Dalit subjectivity in India has been variously represented in regional languages. According to the *Encyclopaedia of Indian Literature, Volume II*, Dalit literature in Telugu 'saw the light of the day long before the advent of Gandhi on the political horizon' and *Malavandra pata* (Song of the Harijans) was published monthly in *Andhra Bharathi* in 1909, comprising an expression of weaker sections and voicing their 'terror and agonies' (Choudhuri 09). In Marathi, similarly, Dalit writing may be dated back to the times of Jyotirao Phule in the nineteenth century. It can be said that intellectual paradigms of thought shape academic endeavors. The academic interest in the Dalit as a subject of subalternity emerged almost simultaneously with Subaltern Studies, in the 1980s. It was during this time that Dalit literature came to be included as part of the syllabi at school and university levels. Recorded as autobiographies articulating the nature of exploitation experienced by Dalits, early Dalit literature was mostly written in vernacular languages and then translated into English and other Indian and foreign languages. In the process, the term 'Dalit' acquired a new meaning. It came to be understood as a consciousness of oppression and exploitation.

Dalit Literature: A Critical Overview

One of the earliest and most significant contributions to Dalit literature in English is *Poisoned Bread: Translations from Modern Marathi Dalit Literature* (1992), edited by Arjun Dangle, a founder member of the Dalit Panthers. The anthology voices the angst and anguish of Dalits, who are denied basic human rights by the upper castes, as a collective consciousness. In his introduction to the volume, Dangle observes that 'Dalit is not a caste but a realization and is related to the experiences, joys and sorrows, and struggles of those in the lowest stratum of the society' (Dangle iii). The volume refers to people who continue to be exploited and oppressed economically, socially, culturally, and in the name of religion and other divisions.

The collection derives its name from a short story by Bandhu Madhav, titled 'Poisoned Bread'. The story narrates the experiences of mahars, a Dalit community, and the continuous humiliation they are subjected to due to age-old casteist prejudices. The story narrates the experiences of the young Mhadeva, the educated grandson of Yetalya Aja, as he recollects his visit to the upper-caste Bapu Patil's house with his grandfather, to look for a winnowing job during the harvest season. Empowered by his caste, Bapu Patil abuses them for belonging to the mahar community and humiliates them. As

Mhadeva retorts to his repeated insults, Bapu Patil replies, 'A Mahar is a Mahar even if he passes LLB and becomes a barrister' (Dangle 169). Unhappy with their work and conduct, Bapu Patil refuses them their rightful share of corn as their wages, despite getting the work done by them. Dejected, Yetalya Aja notices pieces of stale bread lying on the floor. They had turned green and foul, and were smeared with the dung and urine of oxen. He begs Bapu Patil for those crumbs, and that night, they eat those crumbs mixed with *dulli* for supper. Yetalya Aja dies the next day of dysentery and vomiting. In his last moments of agony, he tells Mhadeva, 'Take away this accursed bread from the mouth of the Mahars. This poisonous bread will finally kill the very humanness of man' (Dangle 174). This line resonates in the mind of Mhadeva, the homodiegetic narrator who is witness to the incident, and also in the minds of the readers, and conveys the position of Dalits in the rural agricultural society.

Arjun Dangle's 'Promotion' presents a more complex understanding of the existential crisis faced by a Dalit individual as he finds himself elevated into the 'middle class' by virtue of a promotion attained through reservations. Waghmare, the protagonist of the story, is cornered in the office, despite his seniority, by Godbole who claims caste-superiority. Struggling to assert his individual prosperity above his caste identity, Waghmare is hesitant to even acknowledge a greeting in the name of Ambedkar. When greeted with 'Jai Bheem', he gets 'the feeling of being closely watched by those around' (Dangle 194). The short story explores the character of the social gaze that an individual has to negotiate while coming to terms with his subalternity with respect to his caste. It offers a glimpse into the divisions within Dalit communities, where legal sanction does not yield social acceptance, and those who prosper from within the community aspire to dissociate themselves from the collective caste identity in order to attain social acceptance and respectability.

Another dominant form of Dalit literary expression is poetry, mostly written in blank verse. Poetry, in Dalit literature, is a medium voicing the subjectivity of pain. Quite unlike the traditional expressions of mainstream poetry, Dalit poetry is replete with references to inhuman subjugation, experience of hunger and violence. In his poem 'Hunger', Namdeo Dhasal asks, 'Will hunger-fires forge a poem? / Will music die in the fire of hunger?' (Dangle 50). In a very compact utterance, these lines record a narrative of deprivation and denial. Similarly, one of the earliest poets of Dalit literature in Marathi, Baburao Bagul, examines the hypocrisies of this caste-ridden nation in his poem 'You who have Made the Mistake', and urges those exploited in the name of caste and shunned as untouchables to '. . . either leave the country, / or make war!' (Dangle 81). The idea of war here indicates a subaltern uprising against caste hierarchy.

Unlike the Marathi Dalit poets who deliberately broke away from traditionalist forms of poetry, in Telugu literature, Gurram Jashuva, who raised his voice against the caste system and untouchability, wrote using classical forms. Emerging from his own experiences of oppression based on caste, Jashuva's poetry is filled with pathos. They critique the misery, poverty and deprivation stemming from a social hierarchy of exploitation. In one of his poems, he describes the life of Dalits in the following words: 'if he does not sweat there will be no food for the world, / yet he has no food' (Choudhuri, *EIL Volume II* 24). Jashuva, here, problematises caste hierarchy. Some of his other important works include *Gabbilamu* (1941) and *Kristu charitra* (1958). The latter is the story of the life of Jesus Christ, retold in verse, from an alternative perspective. Jashuva is credited with appropriating classical forms to write Dalit poetry and to voice a Dalit subjectivity.

Autobiographies are also recognised as an important form of expression in Dalit literature. As firsthand accounts or *testimonios* of suffering and exploitation, the autobiography as a genre allows unrestrained recording of facts and emotions without engaging in aesthetic debates. We have already discussed *Karukku* in the previous chapter. Another prominent work is *Viramma: Life of an Untouchable*. Narrating the practice of untouchability in Tamil society, Bama's *Karukku* established the autobiography as a form of Dalit expression in Tamil, when it was published in 1992. Marathi, however, already had a tradition of autobiographies by Dalit writers.

Karukku derives its name from the saw-edged Palmyra leaves which act as double-edged swords, scratching and tearing one's skin. In the author's preface to the first edition, Bama states that the events in her book 'occurred during many stages of my life, cutting me like karukku and making me bleed' (xxiv). Growing up in a village divided into separate spaces assigned to different castes, Bama recollects her encounter with education, class, caste and religion as a child born into a Dalit family. Class, here, emerges as a stable component of the hierarchy of exploitation, which is maintained through upholding caste division so as to ensure that the parayas continue to serve the naickers through generations in lieu of residual food as their pay. Despite policy changes and programmes initiated by the government, the plight of the Dalits does not change. This huge gap between theory and praxis is addressed by the author as she notes, 'there is no way at all for the Dalit who sticks to fair methods, and who toils hard all her life, to make good' (Bama 53).

Similarly, Bama's recollections of her experiences at school and later as a nun, show how power is granted as social sanction to the higher castes who are also from the affluent class. They also prove that education as well as religion, in practice, serve as ideological state apparatuses that stabilise this social hierarchy based on caste. Bama notes that 'the church, the school, the convent and the priest's bungalow were all in places where the upper caste communities lived' (88). Instead of re-forming through interrogation, education reinforces caste divisions and prejudices. Bama recollects how at school 'everyone seemed to think Harijan children were contemptible' and used them for 'cheap labour' so that they 'did all the chores that were needed about the school' (18). Her experience with the Church is no different and she observes that 'they have made use of Dalits who are immersed in ignorance as their capital, set up a big business, and only profited their own castes' (80). Later, her life at the convent as a nun only adds to her experience of discrimination as she notes, 'it is injustice that dances like a demon in the convents, and within all the institutions that are run by these people' (106).

Caste consciousness which leads to caste oppression seems to be imbibed through generations as a hegemonic order maintained within society. Hence, social welfare policies aiming at equality cannot be implemented effectively, since the institutions and people required to implement these are mostly followers of the hegemonic discourse of order based on caste divisions. Shankarrao Kharat's 'A Corpse in the Well' narrates such an episode. The writer witnesses as a child the kind of danger a man from the mahar community is exposed to as his father is asked by the head constable to get inside an abandoned well to remove the corpse spotted floating in it. Full of questions such as 'whose dead body is this anyway? Whose well? Why should my father have to be cursed and threatened because of them?' swarming inside his head, the young boy suddenly spots a snake inside the well moving towards the corpse as his father dangles on the rope hurled into the well (Dangle 88). The episode highlights social discrimination based on caste hierarchy and the predicament of a particular community within the larger narrative of political independence and constitutional equality.

Sharankumar Limbale's 'The Bastard', on the other hand, narrates the story of the turmoil faced by a Dalit child as he comes of age and realises his inheritance of caste. The vulnerability of Dalit women is represented as the writer narrates how his mother is subjected to multiple layers of subjugation on the grounds of caste as well as gender. The recollection ends with an interrogation of this system of social stratification based on endless exploitation of the female body and the impact it has upon the children born of such interactions. Limbale writes, 'Am I a caste-Hindu? But my mother is an untouchable. Am I an untouchable? But my father is a caste-Hindu. I have been tossed apart like Jarasandha – half within society and half outside' (Dangle 142). One cannot miss here the powerful allusion to the mythological king of Magadha who was torn apart by Bhima (at the advice of Krishna) disguised as a brahmin. By alluding to Jarasandha, Limbale weaves within his narrative a subversion of the accepted orders of the mainstream upper-caste system of faith. He provides a contrapuntal reading of the plight of Jarasandha who is otherwise represented as a villain and whose slaying is read as justice attained through divine sanction.

The Outcaste (2003) by Limbale, translated from the original Marathi *Akkarmashi* (1984), presents yet another example of the suffering and oppression faced by Dalits. Written as an autobiography, the book explores the gap between experience and emotion, and verbal representations of these. The episode of a school picnic, recollected by Limbale, narrates prejudices imprinted upon young minds at various levels, and how upper-caste students were asked to collect leftover food to be handed over to the mahars. Later, when the students are asked by the teacher to write an essay on the picnic, the author fails to write as he is weighed down by the traumatic recollections of humiliation and oppression. The story concludes with the question of how the author should begin the essay.

Acquiring education and the emergence of first-generation learners is an important step in recording Dalit utterances. Autobiography and poetry, therefore, serve as preferred genres when it comes to voicing angst or protest. The short story and novel as forms of literary expression, hence, emerge later in Dalit literature. Further, it would be important to remember that in the multilingual context of India, Dalit literatures have existed in various regional languages and had to depend on translations to reach a larger readership. Though Marathi literature provided the first impetus towards the creation of a separate stream termed as Dalit literature, other Indian languages also had been recording these oppressed voices as sporadic works interrupting the mainstream of traditional literature. In the following sections let us take a brief look at Bangla Dalit literature as a case study.

Bangla Dalit Writing

In West Bengal, the beginnings of a separate stream of Dalit literature emerge much later, and they date back to the 1980s and 90s. In her Introduction to *Dalit Lekhika: Women's Writings from Bengal* (2020), Kalyani Thakur Charal, one of the well-known Dalit writers from Bengal, observes that 'in Bengal, caste discrimination is concealed under the shroud of class discrimination' and hence works recording first-person accounts of Dalit experience emerge much later compared to the other languages (Charal and Dasgupta xv). In fact, subjected to various social and political events, such as the Partition of 1947, the people of Bengal were pushed to negotiate continuously with political and economic realities that were constantly changing. Belonging to the lowest order of economic hierarchy, the Dalit population struggled to sustain itself in the face of such events. Hence, the Dalit consciousness in Bangla took longer to form and manifest itself.

A major step in this direction, the Bangiya Dalit Lekhak Sahitya Parishad was formed in 1987, and it organised the first literary event related to Bangla Dalit literature towards the end of the same year. The Bangla Dalit Sahitya Sanstha was formed in 1992 after the death of Chuni Kotal, a girl who was subjected to caste discrimination while pursuing her higher education and committed suicide. Raising her voice against the ruthless violence inflicted upon the caste-oppressed and marginalised people, Chuni Kotal had written in a poem titled 'Mutiny', 'Does this country not have any rules or any courts?' (Charal and Dasgupta 140). Her outraged cry for justice interrogates the mainstream power structure based on the hegemonic inheritance of the caste order. Though her death triggered the formation of a platform to register the raging voice of protest, the visibility of Dalit literature still remained confined to tabloids and little magazines such as *Chaturtho Duniya*, *Atoeb*, *Ekhon Takhon*, *Neer Ritupatra* and *Janajagaran*, to name a few. Of these, *Chaturtho Duniya* was published as the mouthpiece of the Dalit Sahitya Sanstha. One of the major articles credited with bringing Bangla Dalit literature to an English readership is 'Is there Dalit Writing in Bangla?' (2007), by Manoranjan Byapari (translated by Meenakshi Mukherjee). Tracing the origins of Dalit literature in Bangla with reference to the socio-political realities of Bengal, the article charts a history of Dalit literature in Bengal from Matua sahitya (nineteenth century). It observes that the scattered existence of the caste-oppressed communities in Bengal through the post-Partition years did not allow a collective voice to assert itself against the dominant mainstream literary hierarchy in Bangla.

However, with its gradual emergence, Dalit writing in Bangla has manifested itself in diverse genres and forms, such as poetry, autobiography, non-fiction prose, short story and novels. One such novel which has survived as a dominant expression and also been later translated into English is *Titas ekti nodir naam* (*A River Called Titas* 1955), written by Advaita Mallabarman (1914–51). Describing the struggle for sustenance of the malo community, a fishing community dependent on the Titas river for their livelihood, the novel uses the river as a metaphor for the joys and tribulations of the entire community. Other prominent voices in Bangla Dalit literature include Manoranjan Byapari, Kalyani Thakur Charal and Smritikana Howlader, among others. Byapari's autobiography *Itibritte Chandal jiban* (2014) narrates the trauma of a life of deprivation as a child in the refugee camps of West Bengal and Dandakaranya, and of imprisonment in his youth for his involvement in the Naxalite movement. It is in prison that Byapari acquires literacy. His autobiography was translated into English as *Interrogating My Chandal Life: An Autobiography of a Dalit* (2018) by Sipra Mukherjee. Another important figure in Dalit literature in Bangla is Manohar Mouli Biswas. He was influenced by the Marathi Dalit writers during his stay at Nagpur, and came to be acquainted with their movement. A staunch follower of Ambedkar, Biswas's autobiography, *Surviving in My World: Growing Up Dalit in Bengal*, was originally written in Bangla in 2013 and translated into English by Angana Dutta and Jaydeep Sarangi in 2015.

The Aesthetic of Dalit Expression

Dalit literature in Tamil is also a recent phenomenon, and emerges around the 1990s. An important novel of this period is *Koveru kazhudaihal* written by Imayam (V. Annamalai). Originally published in Tamil in 1994, the novel was translated as *Beasts of Burden* (2001) by Lakshmi Holmström. It narrates the story of Arokkyam, a converted Dalit Christian washerwoman who serves the more prosperous and educated members of her own community. In return, she is paid in kind – rice and grains. The novel, which is considered to be a classic of modern Tamil literature, makes use of everyday language to critique dehumanising practices of oppression based on caste. However, it has remained controversial for vividly depicting the divisions and exploitation within the Dalit community.

Another important contribution of Imayam towards the assessment of Dalit literature has been his interrogation of the societal view of Dalit literature and the writers associated with it. In a conference organised in 2017 by the Sahitya Akademi, Imayam observed that there is a distinctive difference in the questions directed towards writers of Dalit literature by academicians and media. He noted that while they pose questions regarding 'the writer's vision of life and literature' to non-Dalit writers, to the Dalit writer their questions are invariably directed towards 'their primary education, family and the suffering they've faced in their life' (Imayam 13). He adds that 'this forces the Dalit writers to adopt the autobiographical mode of narration' and that the social and academic interest in Dalit literature has its origin in a 'mere sympathy for their sufferings' (13). His novel *Koveru kazhudaihal* breaks away from this compelling attribution of a socially desirable form to the corpus of Dalit literature. As a work of fiction written in the form of a third-person narrative, it defies literary categorisation on the basis of caste, and Imayam refuses to be pigeonholed as a Dalit writer.

In fact, one of the debates associated with Dalit literature has been the assessment of the aesthetics involved in Dalit literature. Written in sharp contrast to the established traditionalist mainstream literature, Dalit literature demands an alternative basis of analysis and appreciation. Mostly based on experience, Dalit literature often does not intend to adhere to the yardsticks of literary assessment which are usually applied to mainstream literature. It is this gulf between experience and literary representation that Limbale seeks to address in *Towards an Aesthetics of Dalit Literature* (2004). Limbale states that 'Dalit literature is a movement' and adds that Dalit writers 'see their literature as a vehicle for their pain, sorrow, questions and problems' (105). He argues that one who has not suffered as a Dalit at the hands of the upper castes cannot voice the sense of humiliation experienced by a Dalit, as pain filtered through aesthetics and craft diminishes the anguish associated with it. He argues that Dalit literature, submerged in the experience of pain, must not be evaluated by traditional standards of literary merit, for pain expressed is pain experienced in these personal records of existential humiliation.

Hence, unlike traditional mainstream literature or *savarna* literature, the emphasis in Dalit literature is not on beauty or spirituality. On the contrary, these are literary representations embodying ground realities of dominance and suppression – far away from the abstract realms of literary aestheticism. Marked by an explicit influence of Ambedkarite thoughts and ideals, Dalit literature focuses on the material, unlike traditionalist mainstream literature which seeks beauty in the abstract or the spiritual. Autobiographies and poetry, therefore, assume the highest claim to authenticity in expressing pain. Unfiltered registers of anguish and suffering, these narratives record and convey the experiences which are relevant to all human individuals across all times.

★★★

Dalit literature, read from the perspective of Subaltern Studies, constitutes what can be referred to as 'protest literature' or 'literature of resistance'. Actively engaging with recollections of suffering, trauma and humiliation based on caste, this form of subaltern utterance seeks to interrogate the system of social stratification governed by caste as the determinant. While Marxist ideologies have played a major role in inspiring these writings, especially in certain languages like Telugu, it would be incorrect to argue that Marxist movements were the only causal factor giving rise to Dalit literature. Its emergence in different Indian languages at different points of time can be linked to an array of socio-political events that sparked the need to raise a voice of protest against the dominant caste hierarchy. Though much research is being done in Dalit literature and criticism, there is much more to be done as caste as a component of identity continues to dominate the social life of India.

REFERENCES

Ambedkar, Bhimrao. *Who were the Shudras?*. <https://www.pdfdrive.com/who-were-the-shudras-e43177983.html>.

---. *Annihilation of Caste*. <https://www.google.co.in/books/edition/Annihilation_of_Caste/Eio8BQAAQBAJ?hl =en&gbpv=1&dq= annihilation+of+caste&printsec=frontcover>.

Bama. *Karukku*. Tr. Lakshmi Holmstrom. Oxford UP, 2012.

Biswas, Manohar Mouli. *Surviving in My World: Growing Up Dalit in Bengal*. Tr. Angana Dutta and Jaydeep Sarangi. Bhatkal and Sen, 2015.

Byapari, Manoranjan. *Interrogating My Chandal Life: An Autobiography of a Dalit*. Tr. Sipra Mukherjee. SAGE Publications Pvt Ltd, 2018.

Byapari, Manoranjan. 'Is there Dalit Writing in Bangla?'. Tr. Meenakshi Mukherjee. *Economic and Political Weekly* 42.41 (2007). <https://www.epw.in/journal/2007/41/perspectives/there-dalit-writing-bangla.html>.

Charal, Kalyani Thakur, and Sayantan Dasgupta, ed. *Dalit Lekhika: Women's Writings from Bengal*. STREE, 2020.

Choudhuri, Indra Nath, ed. *Encyclopaedia of Indian Literature (Revised Version) Volume II*. Sahitya Akademi, 2009.

----, ed. *Encyclopaedia of Indian Literature (Revised Version) Volume III*. Sahitya Akademi, 2012.

Dangle, Arjun, ed. *Poisoned Bread: Translations from Modern Marathi Dalit Literature*. Orient Blackswan, 2009.

Dumont, Louis. *The Caste System and Its Implications*. Oxford UP, 1998.

Ghurye, G. S. *Caste and Race in India*. Popular Prakashan, 2004.

Guha, Ramachandra. 'The Rise and Fall of the Term "Harijan"'. *The Telegraph* 10 June 2017. <http://ramachandraguha.in/archives/the-rise-and-fall-of-the-term-harijan-the-telegraph.html>

Guru, Gopal. 'Dalit Movement in Mainstream Sociology'. *Economic and Political Weekly* 28.14 (1993): 570–73. JSTOR, <www.jstor.org/stable/4399553>.

----. 'Dalit Women Talk Differently'. *Economic and Political Weekly* 30.41/42 (1995): 2548–50. JSTOR, <www.jstor.org/stable/4403327>.

Guru, Gopal, and Sundar Sarukkai. *The Cracked Mirror: An Indian Debate on Experience and Theory*. Oxford UP, 2012.

Ilaiah, Kancha. *Why I am Not a Hindu: A Sudra Critique of Hindutva Philosophy, Culture and Political Economy*. SAMYA, 1996.

Imayam. *Beasts of Burden*. Tr. Lakshmi Holmström. Niyogi Books, 2019.

Johnson, Guy B. 'Caste, Class, and Race'. *The Virginia Quarterly Review* 24.3 (1948): 455–59. JSTOR, <www.jstor.org/stable/26440013>.

Kothari, Rita. 'Caste in a Casteless Language?: English as a Language of "Dalit" Expression'. *Economic and Political Weekly* 48.39 (2013): 60–68. JSTOR, <www.jstor.org/stable/23528481>.

Limbale, Sharankumar. *The Outcaste*. Oxford UP, 2003.

----. *Towards an Aesthetic of Dalit Literature*. Orient BlackSwan, 2004.

Lorenzen, David N. *Praises to a Formless God*. Sri Satguru Publications, 1997.

Ludden, David, ed. *Reading Subaltern Studies*. Permanent Black, 2002.

Mallabarman, Advaita. *Titas Ekti Nodir Naam*. NBA Private Limited, 2013.

Phule, Jyotiba Rao. *Gulamgiri*. <https://www.44books.com/gulamgiri-jyotiba-rao-phule.html>.

Purushotham, K. 'Evolution of Telugu Dalit Literature'. *Economic and Political Weekly* 45.22 (2010): 55–63. <https://www.jstor.org/stable/27807079>.

Rege, Sharmila. 'Dalit Women Talk Differently: A Critique of "Difference" and Towards a Dalit Feminist Standpoint Position'. *Economic and Political Weekly* 33.44 (1998): WS39–WS46. JSTOR, <www.jstor.org/stable/4407323>.

The Criminal Tribes Act 1871. <https://ccnmtl.columbia.edu/projects/mmt/ambedkar/web/readings/Simhadri.pdf>.

Tiwari, Badri Narayan. *Documenting Dissent: Contesting Fables, Contesting Memories and Dalit Political Discourse*. Indian Institute of Advanced Studies, 2001.

----. 'Reactivating the Past: Dalits and Memories of 1857'. *Economic and Political Weekly* 42.19 (2007). <https://www.epw.in/journal/2007/19/1857-special-issues-specials/reactivating-past.html>.

Chapter Six

Subaltern Studies in Latin America

In 'Subaltern Studies: Projects for Our Times and their Convergence', Ranajit Guha writes about the expansion of Subaltern Studies as an academic discipline across geographical borders and observes that these two projects – Subaltern Studies in India and that in Latin America – are not bound together or made relevant to each other by territoriality but by temporality. Marginalisation is not an isolated act restricted to cartographic specificities. Hence, in a discussion of Subaltern Studies as an academic approach, it is essential to refer to the Latin American Subaltern Studies Group.

Geographically referring to the entire stretch of land including the nineteen sovereign states from the northern border of Mexico to the southern tip of South America, 'Latin America' has had a socio-cultural history and experience of subjugation in terms of identity determined by race, ethnicity and cultures. The twentieth century witnessed several insurgencies related to land rights in the different countries comprising Latin America, and in the process, they significantly changed the Latin American ideas of nation and its people. According to the 'Founding Statement' of the Latin American Subaltern Studies Group, the concept of the subaltern in Latin America may be understood in the light of the three revolutions which reshaped the political configuration of the territory – the Mexican Revolution (1910–20), the Cuban Revolution (1953–59) and the Nicaraguan Revolutions (1961–90). However, what complicates the concept of Subaltern Studies in Latin America is the fact that Latin American Studies as a separate academic approach had already existed from the 1960s. Hence, the need for redefining the subaltern from a new perspective in the 1990s needed to not only establish its requirement in theoretical and academic terms but also identify the shortcomings of the pre-existing approach, so as to justify the emergence of a new field.

LATIN AMERICAN SUBALTERN REVOLUTIONS

The colonial invasion of the Latin American countries started in the fifteenth and sixteenth centuries, beginning with Christopher Columbus's first journey to America in 1492, and went on till the establishment of a large Spanish empire in Mexico under Hernán Cortés in 1519 and the conquest of the Inca empire by Francisco Pizarro in 1530. Destroying the existing indigenous civilisations of the Aztec, Inca and Mayan empires, the colonisers killed off most of the native population. Yuval Noah Harari notes in *Sapiens* (2011) that 'for the subjugated natives, these colonies were hell on earth' and with the depletion of the native population, 'the Spanish colonists began importing African slaves to fill the vacuum' (326). This resulted in the creation of a feudal state order as the land owners were largely Europeans, and that, in turn, led to the oppression of the indigenous native population, called 'Indians', since Latin America is till date, a largely agriculture-based society.

Though most of the countries of Latin America attained independence in the nineteenth century, the postcolonial nations still followed the oligarchic hierarchy of the past where the societies were dominated by the white criollos who continued to oppress the 'Indians', the population of African descent, and the mestizos and the mulattoes who constituted the peasantry. The Mexican Revolution (from 1910 to 1920) challenged this established order of a white dominated Eurocentric society. It was an armed struggle directed against the policies of Porfirio Diaz, the then President of Mexico, which favoured the wealthy landowners and industrialists. The rebels, strategists and leaders of the revolution belonged to the community of 'Indians' and poor mestizos. However, with the end of the revolution, the subalternised section of the population once again came to be dominated by a newly emergent mestizo upper and middle class, leading to a pattern of class– and ethnicity–based re-subalternisation. In the post-revolution society, the ethnic identity of the 'Indians' became cultural artifacts, while they were denied their right to self-determination and recognition as agents of the revolution.

The Cuban Revolution (from 1954 to 1959) led by Fidel Castro was also an armed revolt of the people directed against the dictatorship of the then Cuban President, Fulgencio Batista. It opposed the US dominance of Cuban sugarcane plantations and the Cuban economy, and aimed at radical agrarian reforms. Inspired by the Marxist ideals, the Cuban revolution brought together the common people as well as the peasants of Cuba. In his speech delivered at the first Latin American Youth Congress in 1960, Che Guevara, one of the important leaders of the Cuban Revolution, noted how the rebellion brought the people from the cities and the peasants of Cuba together, and how 'the children of the cities' learned to respect the peasants, their 'sense of independence' and 'recognise their age-old yearning for the land that had been snatched from them'. He observed that the Revolution was marked by reciprocation: 'the peasants taught us their know-how and we taught the peasants our sense of rebellion'. The success of the Cuban Revolution and the formation of a government led by Fidel Castro redefined the power relations between the US and Cuba, and this led to a partial emergence of the subaltern as the social subject in the decolonised context of Latin America.

The agrarian reforms in Latin America were further shaped by the Guatemalan Civil War which lasted from 1960 to 1996. Triggered by the longstanding issues of unfair land distribution and exploitation of the rural peasantry by European residents who were mostly criollos, and the foreign companies, the Guatemalan Civil War was an uprising led by various leftist rebel groups comprising the indigenous Mayan and Ladino populations against the government of Guatemala. Divided by different political regimes, this period saw a sustained brutalisation and killing of the indigenous people of Guatemala in large numbers through the 1970s and 1980s by forces controlled by the state. The US extended its support to the government and assisted the state in this genocide. The insurgencies in the countryside as well as the city were directed against not just the control of land but also the complete subalternisation of the Mayan and Ladino populations which had led to socio-cultural and political discontent. The Civil War officially concluded with peace negotiations and the signing of peace accords in 1996, including agreements on human rights, indigenous people's rights, and socio-economic and agrarian policies.

The Nicaraguan Revolution lasted from 1978 to 1990. It was initiated along the Marxist lines by the Sandinista National Liberation Front (FSLN) in 1978, against the atrocities of the Somoza dictatorship which perpetuated a semifeudal rural economy of exploitation. The Somoza government was overthrown in 1979 and the Sandinistas assumed control of the state. The Sandinistas initiated several welfare programmes for the general population across the country, such as those related to land reforms, basic necessities, public services and education. However, a phase of violent counter-revolution against the Sandinista government, known as the Contra War, followed (1981–90). It was led by the followers of the Somoza family and supported by the right-wing administration in the US led by President Ronald Reagan. This period is marked by brutal assassinations and human rights violations by the 'Contras'. Along with the Salvadoran Civil War (1979–92), which was also precipitated by the socio-economic inequality in El Salvador, the continuous clashes between the Sandinista and Contra forces in Nicaragua destabilised the entire region during this period.

Ideologically motivated by the Marxist concept of revolution, these series of insurgencies and uprisings shaped the concept of a subalternised Latin American identity through the assertion of cultural differences and indigenous practices. A report on land inequalities in Latin America, titled 'Unearthed: Land, Power and Inequality in Latin America', published by Oxfam International in November 2016, states that one of the main unresolved problems in Latin America continues to be 'the extreme inequality in access to and control over land', and observes that it is the cause as well as the consequence 'of the region's extremely polarized social structures and high levels of poverty and inequality' (Oxfam 10). As discussed, all the aforementioned revolutions – Mexican, Cuban, Guatemalan, Salvadoran and Nicaraguan – which resulted in major political shifts within Latin America, were caused by inequalities related to land ownership and rights over land and agriculture.

THE EVOLUTION OF LATIN AMERICAN STUDIES

Latin American Studies began in the 1960s as an interdisciplinary domain of studies that sought to critique history, social sciences, cultural theory and literature to rediscover the Latin American subaltern as a subject lost in the interstices of mainstream knowledge. It attempted to reconceptualise the relation between people and the nation state with reference to the Latin American uprisings and revolutions. The concept of the subaltern in Latin America therefore predates the formation of the Subaltern Studies Group by Ranajit Guha. The idea of reading history against its grain and the nuances explored by Guha and the other subaltern historians in the formulation of the subaltern as a socio-political subject with reference to class, gender and multiple other markers of individual identity, brought Subaltern Studies in close proximity to the discipline of Latin American Studies and led to the formation of the Latin American Subaltern Studies Group in 1993. In their 'Founding Statement' (1993), the Group notes that 'the constitution of the field itself (and of the Latin American Studies Association as its organizational form) as a necessarily interdisciplinary formation corresponds the way in which the South Asian group conceptualized the subaltern as a subject'.

The success of the Cuban Revolution had not only reformed the socio-economic order of the society, but also initiated cultural and political practices that interrogated the authority of Eurocentric historiography and conceptualised the subaltern people from the working classes as the new subject of representation. A major impetus to this idea was provided by the article 'Caliban: Notes towards a Discussion of Culture in Our America' (1974) by Roberto Fernández Retamar, a Cuban poet and literary critic, written in response to a query from a European journalist who had asked him,

'Does a Latin American Culture exist?' Referring to the figure of Caliban from Shakespeare's *The Tempest* as an anagram of 'Cannibal', Retamar observes, 'I know no other metaphor more expressive of our cultural situation, of our reality' (24). The Europeans invaded their land, brutalised and killed the natives, enslaved the mestizo inhabitants and taught them their language, in the process obliterating their indigenous cultures, their inherent differences and imposing a layer of homogeneity on their identities. Retamar adds that 'to assume our condition as Caliban implies rethinking our history from the *other* side, from the viewpoint of the *other* protagonist' (28). The literary figure of Caliban, therefore, becomes a trope representing the subaltern voices of Latin America, while Ariel, the trusted servant of Prospero, is construed as the colonised intellectual, who now has to choose between serving Prospero (and perpetuating the distorted version of Eurocentric history) or joining Caliban in his struggle for true freedom. Juxtaposing the context of *The Tempest* against the Cuban Revolution and referring to the speeches of Fidel Castro and Che Guevara, Retamar writes that in interpreting the figure of Ariel as the intellectual, he is thinking in 'Gramscian terms, above all of the "traditional" intellectuals: those whom the proletariat, even during the period of transition, must assimilate in the greatest possible number, while it generates its own "organic" intellectuals' (62).

The cultural and literary representation of the Latin American identity trying to formulate an alternative vision of their history and existence had already begun with the 'Latin American Boom' – a literary movement which began in the 1960s and 70s. Some of the major Boom novelists include Julio Cortázar, Mario Vargas Llosa and Gabriel García Márquez. The movement was influenced by the European modernists such as James Joyce and Virginia Woolf on the one hand, and the literary traditions developed by the Argentinian writer Jorge Luis Borges, on the other. Their novels broke away from linear narrations of chronological time and often explored history using the technique of magic realism. Retamar's discourse formulating new ways of conceptualising the Latin American identity had a major influence on the Boom writers, the existing domains of social sciences and also the domain of cultural representations such as films. A major cultural shift in the field of music was initiated by Violeta Parra in Chile and Atahualpa Yupanqui in Argentina in the form of the *nueva trova*, the 'new song', movement in the 1960s and 70s. Initiated as a movement against the cultural dominance of North American music in Latin America, the form soon gained popularity and was used to voice the socially, economically and politically marginalised people of Latin America in popular movements such as the Cuban Revolution which involved large-scale participation by students. However, as far as the literary representations of the Latin American subaltern identity by the Boom novelists were concerned, the authority rested with elite male intellectuals who ascribed a subject-position to the subaltern, and it was mostly framed in terms of class. As the 'Founding Statement' of the Latin American Subaltern Studies Group noted, they 'veiled the disparities of blacks, Indians, Chicanos and women' or even political prisoners, and hence were unable to address subalternity as a multilayered criterion of subjugation.

This dissatisfaction with fictional representations led to the emergence of the testimonio as a new literary form. Testimonios differed from novels as they were based on factual experiences of homodiegetic or first-person narrators. One of the well-known examples is *I, Rigoberta Menchu: An Indian Woman in Guatemala* (1983) describing the experiences of a Mayan woman whose mother, father and brother were murdered by the Guatemalan army and who herself suffered various hardships during the Guatemalan Civil War. The testimonio articulates experiences common to several Indian communities in Latin America during the various insurgencies. It becomes a representative of the collective utterance and assertion of subaltern voices authenticated by first-hand experiences of trauma. The 1970s and 80s were also a time when the domain of Latin American Studies was influenced by the French poststructuralist theory, Gramscian Marxism, Cultural Studies and the heritage of the Frankfurt School, thereby deflecting from the orthodox concepts of Marxism dominant in the 60s. Latin American Studies was expanding to incorporate heteroglossia and dialogism as integral components of the subaltern experience.

LATIN AMERICAN STUDIES AND SUBALTERN STUDIES

It is this critique of the idea of the nation and the national, with reference to the diverse populations of Latin America, which brings Latin American Studies closer to the concept of Subaltern Studies as formulated by Ranajit Guha. The idea of territoriality is redefined when the nation/national is perceived from the subject-positions of different subaltern groups in terms of their individual identity – be it criollos, mestizos, mulattoes, blacks, 'Indians', peasants, proletariat, men or women. The Latin American Subaltern Studies Group conceptualises the subaltern as 'a mutating, migrating subject', and the objective of the Group is to acknowledge 'the presence of this subject' and study 'how they force themselves into the administrative structures and practices of domination as flesh-and-blood living beings'.

Many Latin American scholars were able to find common cause with the Subaltern Studies project being led by Guha. Recollecting the formation of the Latin American Subaltern Studies Group in her article 'How Ranajit Guha Came to Latin American Subaltern Studies' (2005), Patricia Seed writes, 'There we were, a group of academics who knew a lot about politics on the ground in various Latin American countries, and who wanted to think about the different ways in which literature from and about Latin America should be taught and understood – especially from within the United States' (110). However, there were also conflicts with the already existing concept of Latin American Studies and resistance towards accepting Latin American Subaltern Studies as a new domain. In 'Writing in Reverse: On the Project of the Latin American Subaltern Studies Group' (1994), John Beverley recollects how their grant proposal including the 'Founding Statement' for the Group was rejected by the Rockefeller Foundation, and how at various academic platforms such as that of the Latin American Studies Association in Atlanta in 1993, the concept of a new Subaltern Studies Group in Latin America was treated with hostility. It was thought to be a redundant jargonistic repetition of the already explored domains of Latin American Studies that dealt with the plurality of Latin American identities with reference to historical and cultural contexts. Beverley observes that the proposed approach of Subaltern Studies in Latin America identified with the South Asian Group in 'its acute sense of the limitations of elite discourse, whether historiographic, anthropological, or literary' (273). In fact, it went beyond the transcultural approach of Latin American Studies, claiming to represent the subaltern by accepting Guha's proposition that the 'elite discourse and the institutions that contain it, like the university or literature, are themselves complicit in the construction and maintenance of subalternity' (273). The concepts of nation and nationalism which become intricately entwined with the location of the subaltern subject and determine the narrative authority in postcolonial historiography also undergo a change when applied to Latin America. Beverley notes, 'what we have added to the South Asian Group's concern with the "monism" (the phrase is Guha's) of colonial and postcolonial historiography is a postmodernist concern with the effects of the current processes of economic, demographic, and cultural transnationalisation on Latin America' (Beverley 275).

The existing domain of Latin American Studies was deeply influenced by theorists and theories from Europe and the US. The Subaltern Studies Group in Latin America sought to reinvestigate the interstices of overlapping and merging histories, in order to arrive at an approximation of the subaltern's utterance as a politically conscious act informed by individual choice. Ileana Rodriguez, one of the founder members of the Latin American Subaltern Studies Group, notes that 'Latin American subaltern studies aims to be a radical critique of elite cultures, of liberal, bourgeois, and modern epistemologies and projects, and of their different propositions regarding representation of the subaltern' (*The Latin American Subaltern Studies Reader* 09). Connecting with the postcolonial purpose of reinvestigating historiography, as claimed by the Subaltern Studies Group in South Asia, Rodriguez in a later article, 'Is There a Need for Subaltern Studies?' (2005), comments on the contextual difference in postcolonial studies in Latin America: 'In the Latin American version of Postcolonial Studies, there was an explicit validation of ancient Amerindian cultures, a desire to unearth their old epistemological ways of organizing the universe and a desire to validate them' (51).

Such differences in their immediate contexts and their sense of postcoloniality or postcolonial historiography have impeded a close association or a fruitful interaction between the South Asian and the Latin American Subaltern Studies groups. As Rodriguez notes, 'while we did our thing they did theirs, and in so doing, we all remained locked within our own forms of localism. Hence we chose to relate to each other through the European mediation of Antonio Gramsci', thereby defeating the entire purpose of engaging in a collective subaltern discourse by transcending the boundaries of European knowledge and Western thought ('Is There a Need for Subaltern Studies?' 56). Nonetheless, Subaltern Studies in Latin America continues to provide scholars and researchers with a discursive analysis of subalternity as a diverse and slippery subject constructed by hegemonic concepts of history and politics.

SUBALTERNITY IN LATIN AMERICAN LITERATURE

Emerging against the immediate sociopolitical backdrop of the Cuban Revolution and Marxist ideals in the 1960s, the Latin American Boom novelists introduced a new perspective which blended historical consciousness and quest for identity with literary conventions of Western modernism and the indigenous traditions of storytelling. The protagonist in these novels is an inhabitant of Latin America and the point of view is that of an insider. Mostly an experimental genre, the Latin American Boom was a worldwide success as it coincided with the triumph of the Cuban Revolution. The novels written during this time embodied social action and political transitions, and were translated and published by several leading publishing houses across Europe and Asia. One important and immensely popular example is *One Hundred Years of Solitude* (1967) by Gabriel García Márquez.

One Hundred Years of Solitude

In his 1982 Nobel lecture, Márquez addresses at length how the Latin American territory and its people were imagined by the apparently 'rational' West, and provides an account of the violent encounters these foreigners had with the natives. He adds, 'the interpretation of our reality through patterns not our own, serves only to make us ever more unknown, ever less free, ever more solitary'. He rejects such imposed perspectives and replaces them with indigenous ones. Nurtured by this vision and using the technique of magic realism, *One Hundred Years of Solitude* narrates the historical story of seven generations of the Buendía family in a town called Macondo. The town is founded by José Arcadio Buendía, and he perceives the reality of the world outside from his subject position within the town of Macondo. While Márquez claimed that he was creating in his novel a metaphor for Latin America, John Leonard, in his review of the novel, observes that 'Macondo is Latin America in microcosm'. It provides blended narratives of exploitation, struggles, despair and revolution in Latin America through the Buendía family and the town of Macondo. Harold Bloom observes that the journey across the seven generations of the Buendía family is also a journey from the Genesis to the Apocalypse for the world of Macondo: 'it is less a novel than it is a Scripture, the Bible of Macondo' (Bloom 01).

Several incidents are narrated as the novel progresses and the life in Macondo is subjected to multiple changes through its interactions with the world outside. The element of marvel is retained but subverted, because it is no longer the marvel felt by the outer world at the travelogues claiming to have discovered a new land called Macondo, but rather it is the wonder that the Macondonians feel at the claims of progress made by the outer world. The process of 'othering' itself, therefore, stands subverted. The point of view adopted by Márquez is that of an insider. The realities are not defined by existing paradigms of Western thought and rationality; rather, they are coloured by the perceptions of the Macondonians. For instance, when the Macondonians are introduced to Western technology in the form of films, they found it to be an 'outlandish fraud', and the narrator adds that they 'had too many troubles of their own to weep over the acted out misfortunes of imaginary beings' (229). At one level, it is a humorous negation of all dominant European aesthetic claims, but at another level it is also a portrayal of the troubled lives of the people of Macondo and the continuous state of turmoil and imposed invisibility that they suffer.

This invisibility at the socio-economic and political levels is manifested in the novel through a contrast between the dismal lives of the banana plantation workers and that of the rich owners of the banana company. After the company leaves the land and as the fields bereft of rain lay barren and wasted, the narrative of colonial invasion and exploitation is retold from the perspective of the subaltern as the inhabitant and witness to the colonial project of extraction. History repeats itself in Macondo, and as advocated by Retamar, it is narrated in the novel from the perspective of Caliban. The techniques of subaltern communication are intensively used in the novel in the form of rumours and exaggerations – sources which are ignored by mainstream official historiographies. The creation of official archives of hegemonic knowledge sanctified by the power hierarchies, is demonstrated as the workers' strike against the massacre carried out by the banana company is completely erased from the records through the intervention of the state which asserts that 'there were no dead, the satisfied workers had gone back to their families', thereby rendering the subaltern consciousness and the insurgency invisible to history (316).

When Macondo's existence draws to an end, it is the end of an imagined town, despite the realities of the lives that inhabited it or the socio-economic and political situations that it had gone through. In 'The History of Macondo', Gene H. Bell-Villada observes that the chronology of Macondo 'spans from the beginnings of European settlement in America to the dislocations of our time – later sixteenth century to approximately mid-twentieth' (Bloom 39). The detailed family tree at the beginning of the novel is designed to emphasise the actual existence of the Buendía family, and to authenticate the incidents that the narrative would go on to represent. The history of Macondo, as the city itself, is lost in time, but what remains is the story of Macondo as retold by Márquez, attempting to familiarise the reader with the point of view of a plausible subaltern located in the Latin American context.

I, Rigoberta Menchú

Despite its critical acclaim and literary value, *One Hundred Years of Solitude* remains a fictional representation by an elite intellectual with leftist inclinations. With the turbulent changes in the political struggles in Latin America and the continuous state of violence and brutalisation suffered by the natives, especially through the wars and revolutions in El Salvador, Guatemala and Nicaragua and the Contra War, the focus of literary representation shifted from the imagined to the real, from fiction to fact. Consequently, testimonios written by the common people who represented the subalterns who experienced these wars and suffered consequent violence and loss, became more important. One such record is offered by *I, Rigoberta Menchú* (1983), which records the voices of the oppressed indigenous subaltern populations and their narratives of loss and pain. Written as a testimonio, *I, Rigoberta Menchú* is the story of a Guatemalan Quiché Indian woman who loses her family in the struggle for survival against the Guatemalan army, and describes the oppression of the 'Indians' by the ladinos in Guatemala. Menchú, a Guatemalan human rights activist, received the Nobel Peace Prize in 1992.

Representing the marginalised Mayan culture and the Quiché people, Menchú begins her testimonio with, 'I am Rigoberta Menchú. I am twenty-three years old. This is my testimony. I didn't learn it from a book and I didn't learn it alone' (1). In rejecting the 'book' as the source of her knowledge at the very beginning, Menchú categorically rejects the hegemonic dominance of institutional knowledge. It is a rejection of imposed elite versions of mainstream knowledge. The knowledge she acquires is through her life and experiences. She adds that she did not 'learn it alone', and further says that 'my story is the story of all poor Guatemalans' (1). Her testimonio becomes a collective expression of trauma and marginalisation faced by the Mayan people in Guatemala during the Guatemalan Civil War. It becomes a documentation of the subaltern narrative from their point of view, which in turn, challenges the archives of mainstream official historiography.

The testimonio is based in an agrarian society where the land belonging to the family of Rigoberta Menchú is confiscated by the authorities through fraud and deception. Her father is arrested and finally killed as he tries to gather support from the unions. In the fifteenth chapter, as she narrates the episode based around the repeated arrests, torture and harassment of her father which led them to realise as a community the truth about their actual oppressors, Menchú subverts the mainstream idea of entertainment associated with films. She writes, 'Everything in our life is like a film. Constant suffering' (Menchú 15). The scripted unpredictability of the bourgeois form of entertainment is interpreted by the subaltern perspective as a continuously eventful life – where the events are all directed towards their destruction and are therefore, undesirable.

Class and gender play a major role in the testimonio as the Guatemalan Maya woman emerges as an individual doubly marginalised on the basis of these two markers of identity. Apart from the hardships related to poverty that Menchú records in her narrative, the chapter titled 'A Maid in the Capital' provides a detailed account of how young Maya girls were employed in Spanish households. Apart from the inhuman amount of physical labour involved in the household chores, they were often entrusted with the responsibility of initiating the sons of the household 'to do the sexual act', thereby adding gender-based oppression to the oppression based on class (Menchú 9). Further, in the chapter describing the death of Menchú's mother, there is a vivid description of the indigenous protests and their ruthless crushing by the Guatemalan army. Her mother was kidnapped by army men and was repeatedly raped in the army camp by 'the town's high-ranking army officers' and 'officers commanding the troops' (Menchú 25). They subjected her to inhuman physical torture as 'they cut her body bit by bit' and left her 'disfigured and starving', eventually killing her, and even after her death 'the soldiers stood over her and urinated in her mouth' (25). The female body, here, is a site of violence and conquest. Her gendered identity makes her susceptible to physical abuse and sexual torture. Her body was guarded by a sentry to ensure that her community could not claim it. In ensuring such control over the devastated site of conquest, the body becomes an extension of the land which serves as the root cause of the insurgencies.

In an interview published in the *Harvard International Review* in 1994, Menchú says of her book that 'the victims do not choose; they cannot escape the circumstances' and that 'much of what we have lived, however, the international community does not know'. This invisibility of the indigenous people, the lives of the subaltern, acquires articulation in Menchú's testimonio. However, it has been criticised for 'cultural inflation' and generalisation in her celebration of Mayan culture, and also for the descriptions of the violence perpetuated by the Guatemalan army. For instance, Gary H. Gossen observes that 'Rigoberta Menchú's testimony follows a typical rhetorical device of epic narrative: the return of the hero' (67). Gossen approaches the testimonio as 'epic literature' and adds that, it stems from 'Maya sensibilities and story-telling conventions', attempting to assert a Quiché moral and political authority over all other indigenous communities (69). Nonetheless, despite the criticisms, Menchú's testimonio represents the voice of a suppressed community. Defending Menchú, John Beverley argues that the work voices Guatemala's claims as a multilingual and multicultural nation where the 'Indians' 'deserve greater cultural and legal autonomy' and representation in decision making (*Testimonio* 87).

★★★

In the preceding sections we discussed a discernible shift of emphasis in trying to locate the subaltern identity, from the fictional world of Márquez to the narrative of Menchú, or in other words, from the literary form of the novel to that explored by the testimonio. Like the Subaltern Studies Group in India which aimed at reading history against the grain, the Latin American Subaltern Studies scholars too explore the rise of the subaltern voice in multiple contexts of uprisings and the consequent impact on dominant power hierarchies. However, the latter continues to grapple with the idea of postcoloniality as explored by the domain of Latin American Studies. For instance, *Peasant and Nation: The Making of Postcolonial Mexico and Peru* (1995) by Florencia E. Mallon is a postcolonial engagement with the concept of nation and a rewriting of history from the perspective of subaltern participation in the nation. However, the book is not a part of the Subaltern Studies Project. In a later article, 'Subaltern and the Nation' (2005), Mallon recollects that her book was critiqued on the one hand by Latin Americanists for 'lack of attention to empirical detail' and 'overly developed theoretical bent', while on the other hand the members of the Latin American Subaltern Studies Group, such as John Beverley called it a 'biography of the nation' where the historian does not allow the subalterns to speak for themselves but rather 'represents' them in a way that is most functional to the project (1). Mallon, therefore, explores the possible negotiations with the idea of subalternity in the Latin American context which cannot be confined to any single approach. She concludes with the observation that the Subaltern Studies Group in Latin America has at its very core and is defined by a 'contradiction between a modernist yearning for political inclusion, and an equally strong postmodern and postcolonial critique of its limits' (17).

REFERENCES

Beverley, John. 'Writing in Reverse: On the Project of the Latin American Subaltern Studies Group'. *Dispositio* 19.46 (1994): 271–88. JSTOR, <www.jstor.org/stable/41491517>.

----. *Testimonio: On the Politics of Truth*. U of Minnesota P, 2004.

Beverley, John et al., ed. *The Postmodernism Debate in Latin America*. Duke UP, 1995.

Bloom, Harold, ed. *Bloom's Modern Critical Interpretations: One Hundred Years of Solitude*. Bloom's Literary Criticism, 2009.

Gossen, Gary H. 'Rigoberta Menchu and Her Epic Narrative'. *Latin American Perspectives* 26.6 (1999): 64–69. JSTOR, <www.jstor.org/stable/2633926>.

Guevara, Che. 'Speech to the First Latin American Youth Congress', 1960. <https://www.marxists.org/archive/guevara/1960/07/28.htm>.

Harari, Yuval Noah. *Sapiens*. Vintage, 2011.

Latin American Subaltern Studies Group. 'Founding Statement'. *Boundary 2* 20.3 (1993): 110–21. JSTOR, <www.jstor.org/stable/303344>.

Leonard, John. '*One Hundred Years of Solitude*: Myth is Alive in Latin America'. New York Times, 3 March 1970. <https://www.nytimes.com/1970/03/03/archives/books-of-the-times-myth-is-alive-in-latin-america.html>.

Mallon, Florencia E. 'The Promise and Dilemma of Subaltern Studies: Perspectives from Latin American History'. *The American Historical Review* 99.5 (1994): 1491–515. JSTOR, <www.jstor.org/stable/2168386>.

----. *Peasant and Nation: The Making of Postcolonial Mexico and Peru*. U of California P, 1995.

----. 'Subalterns and the Nation'. *Dispositio* 25.52 (2005): 159–78. JSTOR, <www.jstor.org/stable/41491794>.

Márquez, Gabriel García. Nobel Lecture. <https://www.nobelprize.org/prizes/literature/1982/marquez/lecture/>.

----. *One Hundred Years of Solitude*. Penguin Books, 2000.

Menchú, Rigoberta. *I, Rigoberta Menchú: An Indian Woman in Guatemala*. Tr. Ann Wright. Verso, 1984.

----. 'Asserting Our Dignity: The Struggle for Indigenous Peoples' Rights'. *Harvard International Review* 17.1 (1994): 42–79. JSTOR, <www.jstor.org/stable/43661399>.

Oxfam International. 'Unearthed: Land, Power and Inequality in Latin America'. <https://www.oxfam.org/en/research/unearthed-land-power-and-inequality-latin-america>.

Retamar, Roberto Fernández, et al. 'Caliban: Notes towards a Discussion of Culture in Our America'. *The Massachusetts Review* 15.1/2 (1974): 7–72. JSTOR, <www.jstor.org/stable/25088398>.

Rodríguez, Ileana. 'Is There a Need for Subaltern Studies?'. *Dispositio* 25.52 (2005): 43–62. JSTOR, <www.jstor.org/stable/41491786>.

----, ed. *The Latin American Subaltern Studies Reader*. Duke UP, 2001.

Seed, Patricia. 'How Ranajit Guha Came to Latin American Subaltern Studies'. *Dispositio* 25.52 (2005): 107–11. JSTOR, <www.jstor.org/stable/41491790>.

Tum, Rigoberta Menchú, and Georg M. Gugelberger. 'Remembering: The Post-Testimonio Memoirs of Rigoberta Menchú Tum'. *Latin American Perspectives* 25.6 (1998): 62–68. JSTOR, <www.jstor.org/stable/2634208>.

Chapter Seven

Subalternity and Disability Studies

If 'subalternity' is a criterion marked by oppression, dominance, exploitation and denial of basic rights, then the term applies to a significant section of the population pushed to the margins by dominant discourses centred on 'normalcy' – persons with disabilities. An individual's or group's ability to assert its voice is always subject to several markers determining their identity – such as class, gender, race, caste and so on – and depends on multiple social perspectives for recognition. In such a situation, any form of disability, or the presence of an explicit inability in an individual, serves as a major criterion of voicelessness, leading to subalternity. It is important to remember that one of the largest minorities, so to say, in the world is constituted by people with disabilities.

Beginning with a negative prefix – 'dis' – the term 'disability' is a label upon the functionality of an individual. Denoting a lack of something or some capability, the term serves as a comment on competence, and almost automatically generates a response from mainstream society – either in the form of charity or curiosity or stigmatisation. This response is an integral part of mainstream language, culture and life. What is invariably denied to persons with disabilities is the right to self-determination, expression and agency. Construed as 'victims', people with disabilities are subjected to imposed social attitudes, treatment, choices and policies, decided by those that are 'non-disabled'.

In fact, the category identified as 'disabled' undergoes further intrinsic violence as a homogenised comprehension of the term 'disabled' is manufactured and perpetuated by the dominant ableist social order. It is this ableism which assumes that people with disabilities are somewhat inferior to the section comprising people who are non-disabled. It propagates the belief that such people, being inferior, need some kind of a decision regarding their place in the society to be taken on their behalf by the larger majority of 'normal' people. Anita Ghai in 'Engaging with Disability with Postcolonial Theory' (2012) argues that disability as a marker of identity is also subjected to a homogenised interpretation and reframes Spivak's famous question as: 'whether the Subaltern (read disabled) can Speak?' (Ghai 276).

Since the Second World War, Disability Studies has emerged as an area of interdisciplinary research and activism. It seeks to ensure that this section of marginalised population can voice their requirements for themselves and is not denied the right to independent well-being by the larger society.

DEFINING AND ADDRESSING 'DISABILITY'

Disability is defined as 'a physical or mental condition that limits a person's movements, senses, or activities' by the Oxford dictionary. This general definition, however, does not consider the term's possible connection with time or space. A disability, for instance, might be acquired as a result of an accident, or in course of time, such as geriatric restrictions. Similarly, manifestation of a certain disability may be temporary – something which heals with time – or lifelong. In fact, the World Health Organisation states that 'disability is part of being human. Almost everyone will temporarily or permanently experience disability at some point in their life'. Disability, therefore, constitutes a porous category comprising an integral part of the larger society, and is dictated by ableist terms.

People with disabilities have existed across countries and civilisations through centuries, and each society has had its own ways of negotiating this reality. There are various models through which the subject of disability has been perceived and analysed, such as the religious model, the medical model and, more recently, the social model. While the religious model has vacillated between the two extremes of branding disabilities as results of sins committed in one's previous life, to marking the disabled as deserving recipients of charity, the medical model of disability has been dominated by the curative potentials of science and medical research.

From the social perspective, disability has been a marker of exclusion and people with disabilities are not thought of as 'capable' of responsibilities or decision making. With changes in our lifestyle and the growing emphasis on the individual, and the consequent breaking away from a larger concept of family, the discourse of competence and self-sufficiency is associated with the category labelled as 'normal'. This, in turn, brings to prominence the physical hardships faced by people with disabilities and a resultant binary that labels them as 'dependents' or 'liabilities'.

Tracing the social and historical development of perspectives related to disability and the scope of theorising disability in the present context, Lennard Davis notes in his introduction to *The Disability Studies Reader* (2013) that 'the social process of disabling arrived with industrialization and with the set of practices and discourses that are linked to late eighteenth- and nineteenth-century notions of nationality, race, gender, criminality, sexual orientation, and so on' (1). With the advent of industrialisation and capitalist modes of production, the worth of the body came to be determined in terms of productivity related to the individual's ability to work. Hence, the focus now being on the functional abilities of the individual, the collective comprising people with disabilities acquired an almost automatic status of dependents.

The two World Wars in the first half of the twentieth century only added to the numbers in this category termed as 'disabled'. The medical and social requisites for qualifying as 'normal' automatically constituted its binary opposite. With the constitution of the category, 'disabled', the social stigma, sympathy, the idea of inferiority and the consequent presumption of inability towards self-determination were all imposed upon this section, by the dominant discourse of normalcy.

The disability rights movements began in the West – particularly in the USA and UK – as late as the mid-twentieth century. This period saw the coming together of people with disabilities, including the World War II veterans, who demanded alongside the right to independent lives, a review of policies which categorised them as second-class citizens or liabilities. From the 1960s onwards, these movements led to a gradual change in perspectives and policies adopted by governments. Many organisations were formed as collective representations of people with disabilities. The Union of the Physically Impaired Against Segregation (UPIAS), formed in 1972, was one such early disability rights organisation to be formed in the UK. Several bills and acts affecting the lives of people with disabilities were passed and amended in various countries during this time. Some such landmarks in America included The Rehabilitation Act of 1973, the Education for All Handicapped Children Act of 1975, the Individuals with Disabilities Act of 1990, and the Americans with Disabilities Act of 1990. In England, major policy changes initiated by disability rights movements included the Education Act and Disabled Persons Act of 1981, the Disabled Persons (Services, Consultation and Representation) Act of 1986, and the Disability Discrimination Act of 1995 and 2005. Disability movements organised simultaneously across these countries in North America, Australia and Europe led to the development of a discourse conceptualising an equitable society with regard to persons with disabilities.

Along with this activism, the latter half of the twentieth century also saw the rise of new academic approaches and social models that tried to understand disability. In 1948, Ludwig Guttmann organised a competition for wheelchair athletes at the opening ceremony of the Summer Olympics in London. Known as the Stoke-Mandeville Games, it included sixteen men and women who participated in archery. This marked an important social milestone as the Stoke-Mandeville Games later became the Paralympic Games, first held in Rome in 1960. Aimed at inclusion and rehabilitation of people with disabilities, the Paralympic Games is held every four years, along with the Olympics, and the International Paralympic Committee was founded in 1989.

Mike Oliver traces the roots of social models approaching disability to the publication of 'The Fundamental Principles of Disability by the Union of the Physically Impaired Against Segregation (UPIAS)' in 1976. This document clearly distinguished between the terms 'impairment' and 'disability', and stated that it is society that imposes 'disability' upon the physically impaired. Davis, in 'The End of Identity Politics: On Disability as an Unstable Category', further clarifies this distinction by explaining that 'impairment is the physical fact of lacking an arm or a leg. Disability is the social process that turns an impairment into a negative by creating barriers to access' (Davis 265).

In the light of these arguments and with the evolving approaches towards disability – academic as well as social – a major landmark was the United Nation's adoption of the Convention on the Rights of Persons with Disabilities in 2006. With a view to promote equality and eradicate discriminations on the basis of disability, the Preamble describes disability as 'an evolving concept' resulting from 'the interaction between persons with impairments and attitudinal and environmental barriers that hinders their full and effective participation in society on an equal basis with others'. Reiterating the idea that disability is a condition generated by environment and attitudes, besides individual impairments, this formulation follows the social model of disability.

THEORISING DISABILITY

Since identity is a construct formulated by the subject position of the individual, different markers are associated with it through social, cultural, historical and political contexts. Disability is also one such marker construed by the dominant ableist discourse of identity. It is, therefore, like other markers of identity such as gender, class, race, ethnicity and caste, open to analyses from multiple points of view. Disability discourse deals with powerlessness at its core. Denied agency and inclusion, identities of people with disabilities are shaped by existing hegemonic and social prejudices which assume an 'incompetent' subject position for them, in terms of productivity and choice.

Homogenising people with disabilities under a single category is a strategy of oppression. For instance, visual impairment, auditory disability and developmental disorders constitute completely different performative domains and affect the lives of people in very different ways. However, grouping people with such conditions as a collective completely obliterates their individuality and the diversity of their existence by attributing an umbrella term. What is effectively constructed in the process is a binaristic discourse that clearly distinguishes between the 'disabled' and 'non-disabled', granting power to the latter and subalternising the former.

Disability theory is a developing discourse and interrogates powerlessness as a condition imposed on people with disabilities through dominant social and political norms. It explores the concept of disability as a construct through interdisciplinary approaches, because disability as a marker of identity coexists with several other markers like caste, gender, class and race. Hence, disability theory is intersectional. At its core, it merges theories and critical approaches to resist the dominant ableist discourse. It attempts to ensure the inclusion of people with disabilities within the heterogeneous and diverse social fabric.

The postcolonial approach towards disability, for instance, attempts to locate disability within the context of the postcolonial world order. It interrogates the fact that most discourses in disability studies emerge in the West and argues that this silences a large majority of people with disabilities who live in the Global South. Based on a geo-temporal understanding of participation, the postcolonial approach challenges the neo-colonial manifestations at the cultural and discursive levels constituted by Western theories of disability.

Dis/ability Critical Race Studies and Black Disability Studies call for an intersectional analysis of race and disability as connected markers of identity. It is an approach that constitutes 'whiteness' and 'ability' as simultaneous products emanating from the same power position. Feminist theory merges with disability studies to explore gender as an important aspect of constituting the disabled identity. It takes into consideration issues faced by women with disabilities in the dominant ableist and patriarchal structure of society. Crip Theory, similarly, merges queer theory with disability theory. In his Introduction to *Crip Theory: Cultural Signs of Queerness and Disability* (2006), Robert McRuer observes that 'little notice has been taken of the connection between heterosexuality and able-bodied identity' (1). He argues that heteronormativity and able-bodied-ness are interlinked and explores aspects of sexuality in disability studies. It is through these intersectional perspectives that disability studies analyses the construct and representations of disability in literature, films and other forms of expression. However, it is an area of academic interest which needs continuous association with activism because theory and praxis are organically linked in disability studies. Stepping beyond the medical, curative, sensitive and compassionate points of view, disability studies is informed by disability rights movements which seek to ensure all human rights and privileges for people with disabilities.

DISABILITY STUDIES IN THE INDIAN CONTEXT

In the Indian context, the domain related to disability has for the longest time been dominated by the pluralist cultural ethos which forms the complex fabric of its society. Home to multiple religions and cultures – just as the understanding of caste varies from region to region – the approach towards disability in India is varied and is based on socio-religious beliefs and traditions of individual communities. While certain traditions believe that the manifestation of a certain disability is reflective of sins committed in previous birth, most cultural traditions in India agree on sympathy and charity as being the best ways to deal with people with disabilities. As far as care-giving or responsibility is concerned, the normal and obvious flow is always presumed to be unidirectional – that is, from the able to the disabled section – and the latter is automatically kept at the receiving end of patronising acts and attitudes.

Politically, in post-Independence India, policies were adopted to ensure rehabilitation of people with disabilities through welfare schemes and the establishment of the National Council for Handicapped Welfare. With the emergence of disability rights movements in the West, India witnessed an ideological shift in the 1980s. From rehabilitation, the focus shifted to rights and empowerment of people with disabilities. The Rehabilitation Council of India was established in 1986 to address these issues.

However, the movement for disability rights in India may be said to have acquired momentum from the 1990s with the formation of the Disabled Rights Group – a cross-disability advocacy group. A major legislative milestone was attained with the Persons with Disabilities (Equal Opportunities, Protection of Rights and Full Participation) Act of 1995, which was implemented in 1996. This was followed by the National Mental Health Act of 1997, the National Policy for Persons with Disabilities in 2006, and the Rights of Persons with Disabilities Act in 2016.

However, as far as India is concerned, a long standing problem associated with the understanding of disability has been the simultaneous co-existence of poverty – which makes the Indian context very different from that of developed countries of the West. A large section of the Indian population still struggles for basic sustenance, and disability in the Indian context is further problematised by the fact that a majority amongst the people with disabilities are also economically backward. Furthermore, while the West can think in terms of demanding employment and equity for people with disabilities, in India employment itself is a difficult economic terrain to map, even for the mainstream ableist society. Hence, the Western models of disability rights movements cannot be adopted wholesale in the Indian context.

As Renu Addlakha observes, disability studies as an interdisciplinary academic terrain focusing on the contributions, experiences, history and culture of persons with disabilities is yet to emerge in India. Looking at the history, experiences and cultures of individuals with disabilities, disability studies in India as an academic approach tends to seek ways of tracing the existence and subjectivity of these marginalised, silenced and, largely, undocumented people through socio-cultural markers in myths and history, literary representations and subjective experiences.

DEBATES AROUND THE SUBALTERNISED DISABLED

Subalternising people with disabilities is a standard practice in everyday life. Knowingly or unknowingly, words and actions in day-to-day lives sanction this process. If language is a medium of communication, then it is also a conveyor of perspectives and prejudices. Our use of language as expression is shaped by social and cultural conditioning. And discourse is generated and perpetuated through language. As far as referring to people with disabilities is concerned, our language is, more often than not, insensitive if not derogatory. Almost every language has terms to denote specific disabilities.

In *Disability Studies: An Introduction*, Banibrata Mahanta notes that 'negatives are so much a part of the social perception of disability that one is hard pressed to communicate this category in any other form apart from lack' (8). Not just for terms related to people with disabilities, the general use of language in an ableist society encourages – even if unintentionally – a kind of apathy and lacks sensitivity towards disability. It is normal to use expressions such as 'turn a blind eye' or 'turn a deaf ear' or 'provide lame excuses', in everyday use of languages. In the process, the perception of disability as idiomatic and a deliberate choice, if not a ploy, is sanctioned.

Further, the nomenclature to be used for this collective comprising people with disabilities presents a difficulty. Since categorising them on the basis of disability implies the need for a homogeneous group – no matter how diverse the nature of individual impairments might be – the terms used are generic terms which overlook the differences. Moreover, this terminology often ranges from emphasising a 'lack' – such as 'physically challenged', 'physically disabled', 'handicapped' or the more immediate *viklaang* – to being patronising and using unnecessary superlatives such as 'specially-abled' or *divyaang*. Both the variants embody the socio-cultural attitudes towards this subalternised segment of population.

Though 'differently abled' – a phrase coined in the early 1980s by the United States National Democratic Committee in its Manifesto – had gained popular consensus with its apparent thrust on ability instead of lack of ability, the term is presently considered as condescending and hence, inappropriate. In its recognition of ability through difference, it implicates almost the entire human population – as each individual may be said to be differently abled. It does not, therefore, necessarily imply a categorical classification for persons with disabilities, against the non-disabled persons. In fact, even the use of the phrase 'disabled people' semantically focuses on the disability more than the subjective existence of the individuals labelled thus. The phrase 'people with disabilities' prioritises, on the other hand, the 'people' before the 'disabilities'.

Cultural representations of people with disabilities in mythology and ancient legends also shape the manner in which disability is perceived in a society. For instance, in mythologies across the world – ranging from the Greek and Roman to the Indian texts – physical impairments have mostly been presented or interpreted as flawed nature or indication of moral failure. Well-known examples may include Manthara, the hunchbacked maid in the *Ramayana*, or Shakuni, the king of Gandhara, who is represented as walking with a limp in the *Mahabharata*. The cultural stigmatisation is so intense in both the cases that the names Manthara and Shakuni have become negative signifiers and have remained so even in the present times.

As Nandini Ghosh has argued, disability may be 'conceived as being embedded in a particular social context' and it should then be 'interpreted in terms of oppression, keeping in mind other identity markers such as caste, class, gender, sexuality, religion, ethnicity etc' (6). For instance, in the context of the two characters cited above, one would notice how Shakuni – a man in a patriarchal society as well as a king in terms of social hierarchy – has a conjectural counter-narrative attributed to him. This narrative is based on a possible revenge he had plotted against the Kurus as a clan, for marrying his sister Gandhari to the blind king Dhritarashtra. The counter-narrative, hence, serves the purpose of restoring respectability to Shakuni's subject position as a loving brother. However, as far as Manthara is concerned – the poor hunchbacked maid to the mythological queen Kaikeyi – no such counter-narrative has emerged – perhaps because her social position as a representative of the working class and, further, that of a woman, does not require any other explanation except that it was her deformity which led to her evil conspiracy.

In fact, as far as mythology is concerned, one may come across several such representations. These ideas are further consolidated by mainstream media as these myths are enacted and re-enacted to form an integral component of the collective subconscious. This, in turn, generates a process of othering which excludes people with disabilities from the domain of decision-making. Such exclusionary approaches towards people with disabilities as the other is universal to the various groups identified under Subaltern Studies, making it an area of interdisciplinary research attempting to locate historically and socially obliterated subject positions.

As discussed above, disability studies engages with postmodernism, race theory and feminist discourses. Gender as a criterion for subalternity has already been discussed in the third chapter. Disability adds a further layer of subjugation in the context of women with disabilities. An important work in this direction is Anita Ghai's *(Dis)Embodied Form: Issues of Disabled Women* (2003) which provides analyses of cultural constructs around disability and particularly envisions a more inclusive variant of feminism which would include women with disabilities.

THE LITERATURE OF DISABILITY

Disability has had varied literary representations. Writers have often used it as a trope in fictional representations of characters with disabilities. Some use it in an oblique way, instead of making it the centre of the narrative. It is often used as a metaphor depicting passivity, as characters with disabilities are shown as striving to cope with things that happen to them; or sometimes, as markers or peripheral references that assist the progress of the narrative. Some such works in the Indian context would include *The Circle of Reason* by Amitav Ghosh, *Midnight's Children* by Salman Rushdie and *Clear Light of Day* by Anita Desai.

While *The Circle of Reason* narrates the story of Nachiketa Bose, the young weaver also known as Alu (potato) because of his large bumpy head, *Midnight's Children* explores a magic-realist narrative using the trope of special abilities that are bestowed upon children born closest to the stroke of midnight on 15 August 1947. In Desai's *Clear Light of Day*, Baba – the youngest sibling with developmental disorders – is not explored as a character; he, rather, serves as a medium for contrasting the priorities of Tara and Bimla, in terms of commitment and responsibility. These novels, though they directly include the subject of disability, do not explore it in terms of voicing oppression or dominance, or contesting mainstream formulations and attitudes.

In fact, disability in these novels is a peripheral subject. For instance, in *The Circle of Reason*, Alu's head is of little consequence to the development of the plot or to things that happen to him in the course of the novel. It is a visible mark of identification, but the character could have managed without it – as far the plot is concerned. Similarly, in *Midnight's Children*, the focus is on the exploration of the journey of India as a nation since Independence through an emerging postcolonial consciousness. The special abilities are additional abilities, to be read as integral to the allegorical narrative of the nation attempted in the novel, and though they play a role in the development and progress of the plot, it is a literary tool in the hands of the novelist.

In this respect, the treatment of disability in Desai's *Clear Light of Day* is interesting. The existence of Baba – the character with disability in the novel – is meant to highlight the sense of responsibility in Bimla. His existence in the novel is intended to stress the idea of care-giving and commitment. In the process, Baba becomes a signifier of a duty which needs to be accomplished, and Bimla's dedication upholds her morally virtuous position. However, Baba remains a flat character at the receiving end of sympathy and care – from Bimla and the readers alike. He is a part of the larger concern of the novel which primarily deals with themes of family and relationships. His subjectivity is of little importance to the incidents that take place around him.

It is from this perspective that writings about people with disabilities is very different from writings by people with disabilities. While the former provides a sympathetic treatment of the subject of disability, portrays persons with disabilities as receivers of care and nurturing, and uses the theme for some other motive in the work, the latter emerges from an experiential understanding of disability, focuses on the social gaze and offers alternative perspectives to cope with it. The emphasis is on claiming dignity, instead of sympathy, and upholding the need for sensitisation.

Autobiographical writings also record experiences of negotiating society as an individual with disabilities. A well-known example is Helen Keller's *The Story of My Life*, first published in 1903. Recollecting the disease which deprived her of vision and auditory perceptions, Keller writes that this illness 'plunged me into the unconsciousness of a new-born baby' (06). The account traces a gradual re-learning of communication and life skills with the support of her teacher, Anne Sullivan. As a form, the autobiography perhaps provides liberation from the dominant hierarchical claustrophobia of dependence constructed by the social order.

Through the twentieth century which saw the emergence of disability rights movements and activists, the discourse around experiencing physical disability, and also the literature voicing disability, underwent a marked shift in perspective. Instead of narrating the story of disability as a struggle and discussing coping techniques, the later literature of disability tends to accept disability as a challenge but acknowledges the role of science and technology in developing gadgets such as electric wheelchairs or Cannon Communicators which enable people with disabilities to aspire to a life based on choice and self-determination.

A noteworthy instance is *Life Without Limits* (2010) by Nick Vujicic. Born without arms or legs, Vujicic is an internationally acclaimed motivational speaker. He lives an independent life, travels and lectures worldwide. He is the founder of Life Without Limbs, a nonprofit organisation, and writes about the physical and emotional challenges he had to face with his 'abbreviated body' (Vujicic 15). He describes the role played by his family and their acceptance and handling of disability as a physical fact and not an overwhelming trauma. He has set an example by living a life of self-dependence, and Vujicic's videos on YouTube have millions of followers. He explains that 'people are drawn to watch it because despite my physical limitations, I'm living as though I have no limits' (Vujicic 01).

This celebration of life as an opportunity despite physical limitations is an important characteristic of autobiographical writing related to disability. Here, the social gaze of sympathy is replaced by the obvious human right to self-determination and claims of equity. Disability is no longer a peripheral concern – it is a reality as experienced by the marginalised other. The narrator, in the process of explicating his/her life, interrogates the socially ingrained ideas related to physical disabilities. The conventional social understanding of disability is problematised as the writer provides an experiential description of othering which people with disabilities have to confront at various stages of life. Some important recent works in this area include *One Little Finger* by Malini Chib, and *The Other Senses* and *Flight Without Sight* by Preeti Monga.

One Little Finger (2011) is an autobiographical narrative by Malini Chib who has cerebral palsy. Narrating her story from the moment of her birth when the doctor had declared that she would not survive for more than seventy-two hours, Chib asserts, 'I survived' (03). Her experience of trauma is described as she recollects her treatment at a leading children's hospital in Mumbai: 'To them, I was a non-thinking person who needed fixing and fitting into the mould of being normal' (16). Overcoming social gaze and social stigma, Chib types out her book with her one functional little finger and tells her readers how she has 'used the one little finger 250,000 times' (193).

Chib's narrative is important in several ways. Born in Kolkata and then having acquired her primary education at a 'special school' in England, Chib returned to India when she was seven years old. The shock experienced by her as a child at the social insensitivity and ignorance regarding disability in India, in contrast to England, reveals how disability and persons with disabilities are treated in India. For instance, Chib writes of 'special education' in India as being detrimental to the intellectual progress of children with disabilities, and recalls that 'we were perceived as a new breed of people who were praised for whatever we did' (22). Similarly, of the social gaze that treated people with disabilities as social outcastes, Chib writes, 'Indians seem to have made staring a national habit' (196). Another significant point made in her autobiography is the recognition of class as an important factor in determining the opportunities for a person with disability in India. Though that may hold true for other countries as well, Chib discusses how in India, particularly, there was no sympathetic understanding of disability around the time she was born (in the late 1960s) and admits, 'I was fortunate that I came from a privileged and well educated family' (07). Due to her privileged class position, she could access scientific gadgets like the Cannon Communicator and electronic wheelchairs and avail herself of opportunities to education and assessment in England. *One Little Finger* also serves as a critique of the social model of disability in India. Chib writes of her life in London, contrasting it with that in India: 'I do not feel so disabled there. I am independent' (195).

A leading disability rights activist, Chib is the founder and co-chairperson of the non-profit and non-governmental organisation Able Disabled All People Together (ADAPT). It was initially started in 1972 in Bombay by her mother Mithu Alur as The Spastics Society of India. The 2014 film *Margarita with a Straw* which earned critical acclaim is based on the life of Malini Chib.

The Other Senses (2012) by Preeti Monga is the story of a visually challenged aerobics trainer who had lost her eyesight to optic atrophy when she was thirteen years old. Recounting her childhood and the period when the diagnosis occurred, Monga writes, 'I seem to have been transformed into a strange pitiful object to be handled with extra consideration or simply left alone' (30). Monga established an NGO called Silver Linings in 2010 and received a national award in 2013 for her relentless efforts at empowering people with disabilities. In her *Flight Without Sight* (2018), Monga recollects how she started 'trying to make a difference in the quality of life of people with disabilities' (153). She is also a member of the governing council for The Skill Council for Persons with Disability formed by the Ministry of Social Justice and Empowerment.

Another noteworthy work is *River of Time* (2017) by Jeeja Ghosh who has cerebral palsy and is an eminent disability rights activist. A collection of thirty poems, *River of Time* voices subjective responses of the writer towards various events in her life and in society. Just as there are poems like 'Touch' and 'Cloud', resonating with personal experiences, the volume also includes a poem written as a tribute to Nirbhaya – voicing the angst of all human beings, irrespective of the 'ability'-divide. In fact, poetry, as a genre of literary expression, allows space to break free from set patterns of majoritarian mainstream societal norms.

★★★

People with disabilities constitute perhaps the most marginalised section of the population even in the present times. Though there has been a sustained effort on the part of disability rights movements and groups to achieve social equality, the actual realisation of the goal is still a distant dream. A number of laws have been introduced and there have been various initiatives at the institutional level – such as the observance of 3 December as the International Day of Persons with Disabilities since 1992, in order to enable a better understanding of disability and ensure rights to promote the wellbeing of persons with disabilities. However, the social stigma associated with disability still demands a strong critique at individual and collective levels, so that these institutional goals can be realised. We need to frame policies which allow people with disabilities right to self-determination, instead of perpetuating the cultural practice of charity and sympathy. Perhaps the emergence of more voices in disability literature and sustained research in disability studies will ensure that this active process of continuous and explicit subalternisation is brought to an end.

REFERENCES

Addlakha, Renu, ed. *Disability Studies in India: Global Discourses, Local Realities*. Routledge, 2013.

Chib, Malini. *One Little Finger*. SAGE, 2011.

Davis, Lennard J., ed. *The Disability Studies Reader*. Routledge, 2013.

Desai, Anita. *Clear Light of Day*. Vintage Books, 2001.

Ghai, Anita. *(Dis)Embodied Form: Issues of Disabled Women*. Shakti Publications, 2003.

Ghai, Anita. 'Engaging with Disability with Postcolonial Theory'. *Disability and Social Theory: New Developments and Directions*. Ed. Dan Goodley, Bill Hughes and Lennard Davis. Palgrave Macmillan, 2012. 270–86.

Ghosh, Amitav. *The Circle of Reason*. Ravi Dayal Publishers and Permanent Black, 2003.

Ghosh, Nandini, ed. *Interrogating Disability in India: Theory and Practice.* Springer, 2016.

Ghosh, Jeeja. *River of Time.* Power Publishers, 2017.

Keller, Helen. *The Story of My Life.* Cosimo Inc., 2009.

Mahanta, Banibrata. *Disability Studies: An Introduction.* Yking Books, 2017.

McRuer, Robert. *Crip Theory: Cultural Signs of Queerness and Disability.* New York UP, 2006.

Monga, Preeti. *The Other Senses.* Roli Books, 2012.

----. *Flight Without Sight.* Hay House Publishers (India) Pvt. Ltd., 2018.

Oliver, Mike. 'The Social Model In Action: If I had a Hammer?'. *Implementing the Social Model of Disability: Theory and Research.* Ed. Colin Barnes and Geoff Mercer. The Disability Press, 2004.

Stanford Encyvlopedia of Philosophy. <https://plato.stanford.edu/entries/disability-critical/>.

'River of Time: A collection of poems by Jeeja Ghosh'. *India Blooms News Service.* <https://www.indiablooms.com/life-details/LIT/2893/river-of-time-a-collection-of-poems-by-jeeja-ghosh.html>.

Rushdie, Salman. *Midnight's Children.* Penguin, 1991.

Vujicic, Nick. *Life Without Limits.* Waterbrook, 2020.

Chapter Eight

Extending the Boundaries
BORDERLANDS AND MULTIPLE WORLDS

Subalternity is a multidimensional concept. It may be located from various perspectives and through multiple markers of identity such as nation, class, caste, race, disability and gender, to name a few. However, the very premise of voicing subalternity presumes a spatial context, a location – i.e., the individual or group must belong to a specific piece of land, a recognised state. Subaltern Studies as a theoretical approach in postcolonial historiography seeks to retrieve the suppressed voices within an existent mainstream documentation of nationalist history. But when the individual belongs to the borderlands or undefined or contested territorial spaces unclaimed by a state or claimed by more than one state simultaneously, the very idea of subjecthood undergoes a massive change. Since such a space does not have claims to a recognised nationhood, its history as well as that of its inhabitants – largely unknown and undocumented – do not form part of a larger distinct narrative. This gives rise to a 'borderlands perspective' which emerges as a blend of postcolonialism and Subaltern Studies, challenging and interrogating mainstream hegemonic knowledge.

Further, with the emergence of micronations and ideas of a Fourth, Fifth and Sixth World, many ethnic groups and communities that defy the mainstream definitions of the nation, have asserted their existence. Perhaps, in the present scenario, there is an intense need to accommodate these utterances and claims as culture-specific markers of undefined and displaced subalternity. Moreover, in such cases, subaltern voices have hardly any recognition or archival references. Tales of survival are largely oral, localised and anecdotal. Sometimes, evidences of existence find representation in community-based artefacts. Struggling against the fundamentalist mission of homogenising identity, such lives and utterances assert their existence in the day-to-day realities which survive over generations in the form of non-literary evidences.

NATIONS, BORDERS AND SUBALTERNITY

To imagine 'land', one needs to consider 'borders', and borders are known to be porous. Though in terms of theory and cartography, they might serve as distinct markers of territoriality, in practice and in the lives of the people living on these porous margins, they serve as a source of ambiguity with respect to individual and national identities and, consequently, become the site of oppression and marginalisation. Amritjit Singh and Peter Schmidt, emphasising race and ethnicity as crucial markers of individual identity, define borders as 'a part and yet apart, home and not-home, neither "here", nor "there"' (7). As nation states define their boundaries, asserting one's own authority and contesting the claims of the other, there emerge pockets of human population caught in minute pieces of land which are not acknowledged on paper or are rendered invisible by the politics of marginalisation deployed by the 'mainland'. An example of the former situation may be found in the inhabitants of territories marked as 'No Man's Land'. Associated with the First World War, the term is used to refer to a contested or disputed piece of land, located between two nation states, which neither claims as its own for fear of disrupting peace with the neighbouring country.

Internationally, such spaces exist between several states – such as the Korean Demilitarised Zone between North and South Korea; the Golan Heights between Israel and Syria; and Varosha, the 'ghost town' between Cyprus and Turkish-occupied Northern Cyprus. While certain examples of no man's land are uninhabited, there are also those which have human populations residing in them. These people, unrecognised by any of the adjoining nations, lack an acknowledged citizenship; and denial of citizenship implies denial of existence. Their cultures, voices and identities are hence rendered invisible by mainstream historiographies. An example of this in the Indian context may be found in the case of the inhabitants of *chhitmahal*. The term *chhitmahal* refers to pockets of land located in Bangladesh and the Indian states of West Bengal, Assam, Tripura and Meghalaya. The national identity of these spaces was determined, at the political level, by granting of citizenship to people living in specific areas by India and Bangladesh, as late as in 2015.

Another important instance of perpetual postcolonial subalternisation in India may be seen in the context of Kashmir. Kashmir, claimed by both India and Pakistan, has gone through various phases of governance and political regimes. Peace, as a concept signifying the absence of conflict, has been a rare state of existence for the people of Kashmir. Dependent on trade and tourism with both the countries, the economy of Kashmir has always been subject to the underlying threat of unresolved conflicts. Consequently, the infrastructural and technological developments in the area have also suffered, while the residents have had their right to self-determination interrupted by state policies. The case of Kashmir remains a glaring example of postcolonial subalternisation.

One more significant example of marginalisation along the borders may be seen in the case of the north-eastern states of India. Exoticised through systematic homogenisation as the 'seven sister states', the states of Assam, Tripura, Meghalaya, Mizoram, Nagaland, Manipur, Sikkim and Arunachal Pradesh have diverse cultures and are home to people from different ethnic groups, linguistic identities and cultures. Even within the same state, such as Nagaland or Arunachal Pradesh, there are people from different communities and backgrounds residing together. Yet, their connection with the mainland is mostly through an exotic homogenised image which obliterates the intrinsic diversity of the region. Due to topographical and political challenges, these states are yet to evolve adequate infrastructure in terms of health, education, and other basic amenities. Inhabitants of the mainland know little about their native cultures and languages, and the people of these seven states, more often than not, are subjected to the politics of marginalisation and segregation.

Apart from borders and no man's land, there are other locations that do not feature in the matrix of formal negotiations of borders and are nonetheless home to human populations. One such example may be found in the lives of people residing in the ridges formed by various rivers. Since the formation and sustenance of a ridge is determined by the natural dynamics of the river, in terms of territoriality, the piece of land emerging as a ridge becomes the property of the river; and the lives of the people residing therein technically do not fall under the jurisdiction of any administrative hierarchy and therefore, do not form part of any nationalised narratives. The ethnicities, races and cultures of these people find expression by virtue of their interactions with those living on the mainland, mainly through trade and commerce, but their lives and livelihood remain uncharted by mainstream records and official surveys. India, as a land of rivers, has several such ridges formed in various states such as Assam and West Bengal, which are characterised by their impermanence and uncertainties.

In the Latin American context, the borders reinforced into the social fabric by the Mexican, Cuban and Nicaraguan revolutions redefined identities, and interrogated the idea of a homogenised nationality despite varying ethnicities, especially with reference to the Mexicanos, Chicanos and Hispanics. Stressing the need to recognise and record the diversities of the Latin American identity, Ileana Rodríguez asserts 'the necessity for imagining and theorizing Latin American Otherwise is more than a scholarly imperative. It is mainly an intellectual, ethical and political necessity' (xii). The voices of the subalternised population need to be recognised as part of acknowledging human rights and human existence.

The evolving concepts of the micronation and the theory of multiple Worlds further problematise the identification of the subaltern. Defined as an entity which claims to be an independent state but whose sovereignty is not recognised by the international community, the concept of 'micronation' developed in the twentieth century. Well known examples include the Principality of Seborga – a cartographically acknowledged small village on the border of France and Italy which proclaimed itself an independent nation in 1963 – and the Principality of Sealand – a fort in the North Sea off the coast of England abandoned by the British Royal Navy in the 1950s and occupied by the family of Patrick Roy Bates since 1967. Lacking international acknowledgement as a nation, the lives of the people inhabiting these spaces remain unrecorded and thereby constitute subalternity through complete denial of national identity. Similarly, identified as 'least developed countries', the Fourth, Fifth and Sixth World countries are subjected to marginalisation in terms of their political as well as cultural identity by the more developed countries that constitute the international order of political hierarchy.

The primary problem with the mapping of subalternity as constituted in these cases is the availability of records. Theoretically, Subaltern Studies as a postcolonial approach presumes the existence of certain archives or records which subsume the existence of the subaltern subject within the mainstream documentation and thereby deny voice to the subaltern. The subaltern subjectivity, as discussed by Ranajit Guha in *Subaltern Studies, Volume II* (1983), is constituted by primary, secondary and tertiary discourses. However, since the primary and secondary discourses are dependent on official records and documents, in the case of people belonging to the borderlands and multiple Worlds, such official documents mostly do not exist in mainstream records. The study of subalternity in such cases is, therefore, based on the tertiary discourse constituted by the non-official accounts which retrieve subaltern voices and present them to readers in an alternative axis of space and time. Such repositories are provided by alternative archives generated through literatures – oral and written – anthropology, culture studies and other such non-historical domains of knowledge. More often than not recorded in native languages, the retrieval of the subaltern as a subject from these accounts depends on original research and translation to reach a wider readership.

Gyanendra Pandey has discussed how official historiography in India strives to exclude violence arising out of resistance against the state-centred drive for homogenisation within the space of the postcolonial nation state as sporadic incidents, distinct from the flow of an uninterrupted narrative of mainstream history. Pandey notes that 'the "fragments" of Indian society – the smaller religious and caste communities, tribal sections, industrial workers, activist women's groups, all of which might be said to represent "minority" cultures and practices – have been expected to fall in line with the "mainstream" (Brahmanical Hindu, consumerist) national culture', and adds that this 'mainstream', in reality, 'represents in fact a small section of the society' which has 'been flaunted as the national culture' (28). He asserts that in order to challenge official historiography and reclaim those 'contested spaces' documenting the subaltern utterance, it is important to turn to 'what the historians call a "fragment" – a weaver's diary, a collection of poems by an unknown poet' or the 'creation myths and women's songs, family genealogies, and local traditions of history' (50).

Of Indo-Bangladesh Enclaves/*Chhitmahal*

Nationalist historiography presupposes the existence of a nation. However, for people lacking a national identity, nationalist documentations of history hold no validity for their lives or existence. An instance of this denial is found in the case of people inhabiting spaces which have not been recognised by any nation state. In the context of India, the *chhitmahal* or the India-Bangladesh enclaves provide such an example. When the cartographic lines were drawn segregating India, Pakistan and Bangladesh (then East Pakistan) as separate nations, these enclaves came to be divided by the maps in such a manner that pockets of Indian population were included within the map of Bangladesh, and vice versa. As a result, the people inhabiting these lands became refugees – as per postcolonial definitions – without undergoing any kind of geographical displacement at all. The impact of this historical irony was suffered by these people in the form of an outright denial of all human rights and lack of any access to public services or infrastructure such as health, education, and law and order, till a final solution was arrived at and citizenship was granted to them by India and Bangladesh in 2015.

Life in *chhitmahal* has formed the subject of several fictional works written in India as well as Bangladesh. One of the important works based on *chhitmahal* in recent times is *Kumari megher desh chai* (2018) written by Amar Mitra. Loosely translating as 'The Maiden Cloud's Quest for a Home', the title of the novel uses a pun on the word '*desh*' which might signify 'land', 'nation' as well as the sense of security associated with 'home'. In his Preface, Mitra notes that his motive in the novel is to explore the authenticity of the historical claims and controversies regarding the space. The novel merges narratives of agonising daily experiences of people residing in these enclaves with occasional references to historical debates about the space.

On one hand, Mitra's novel traces the parallel journeys of Heratun Dai – mother of Fatima who falls victim to human trafficking – and that of Jaba's mother whose daughter has gone missing, as they helplessly look for their lost daughters who are not, and cannot be, registered as missing by the local authorities as they are not citizens of the country which includes their village within its cartographic territory. On the other hand, it tells the story of Sagir Ali. Ali is over hundred years old and has witnessed the long journey of this village called Mashaldanga, and lives with the dream of casting his vote as a recognised citizen of India. Considerable work on *chhitmahal* was done by the Department of Comparative Literature, Jadavpur University, Kolkata, in 2017. Transcriptions of the audio files documenting these interviews are available on the website of Goethe Institut, Kolkata.

Of the Ridges

A similar problematisation of the subaltern population residing in the ridges formed by river is provided by Kumar Ajit Dutta's Bangla novel titled *Maranya charer itikatha*, published first in 2016 and later revised in 2019. Based on the lives of the people residing in an imaginary ridge in the Brahmaputra, the novel narrates the story of the protagonist Ulfat who acquires education as a graduate in the mainland and then returns to the ridge where he was born to enlighten his people with the knowledge and understanding of exploitation, and to serve the poor. Caught in the throes of superstitions such as pacification of ghosts and spirits before venturing into the river for fishing, the people of the ridge lead simple lives that lack the conceptual apparatus to comprehend state-enforced exploitation. They interact with the mainland at the local bazaars where they come to trade, they pay their taxes to the nation and yet do not feature on the list of development programmes related to the improvement of infrastructure or the quality of lives initiated by the government. Their lives are subject to constant threats of subjugation by state-power on the one hand and destruction by natural calamities such as high tides and floods, on the other. Ulfat's vision of enlightenment inspired by urban concepts of education, therefore, makes little sense to them.

In his Preface to the novel, Dutta elaborates on how the lives of these people remain shrouded in obscurity from the perspectives of mainstream nationalist history. His interactions with the small traders coming from different ridges to sell their goods at the local bazaars in the villages reveal to him their pasts, their lives, their sorrows and the nature of continuous exploitation faced by them, and this, in turn, forms the subject for his novel. He authenticates the subjectivity of these marginalised people by making them speak in a dialect which is a blend of Mymensinghia (the dialect spoken in Mymensingh, Bangladesh) and Assamese. This establishes their socio-cultural identity because historically, during the colonial regime, the British administration had persuaded large numbers of Muslims from Mymensingh to cultivate the barren lands in the areas adjoining the Brahmaputra. The language spoken by the natives in the novel, therefore, becomes the first articulation of disintegration from the mainland and assertion of the existence of a marginalised community.

Of North-east India

In fact, assertion of identity through linguistic distinctiveness forms a major component of registering resistance against ethno-linguistic marginalisation. This is also seen in the literatures of the north-eastern states of India, which constitute a significant part of the Indian borders with neighbouring countries. Suniti Kumar Chatterji describes India as a country of multi-racial, multilingual and multi-religious diversity and notes how throughout history there has been 'a great tendency towards an integration of these diverse elements' under a homogeneous category called 'pan Indian' (5). He categorises the racio-linguistic groups in India as the Austric, the Sino-Tibetan, the Dravidian and the Aryan, and traces the development of Indian bhashas as branches originating from these four groups. Of the Sino-Tibetan family, he notes the development of the Tibeto-Burman branch of languages which are spoken all through the sub-Himalayan tracts, and observes that most of these languages have no written literature but are replete with a wealth of oral literatures in the form of 'some songs and poems, religious and otherwise, and some folk-tales, stories and legends in prose' (8). It is a reaffirmation of Chatterji's observation that one comes across in the literatures from north-east India. Characterised by their ethnolinguistic sharing across borders, the indigenous populations in the north-eastern states of India do not share much of a cultural affinity with the heartland. The diversity in their religious, cultural, ethnic and linguistic identities is denied in characterising them as the 'seven sister states'. Historically, there has been a long postcolonial tradition of armed insurgencies against the federal state in some of these areas. For instance, the Mizo National Front in 1966 launched an armed insurrection against India, claiming an independent state of Mizoram. Similarly, the National Socialist Council of Nagalim comprehends the history and identity of the Nagas as distinct from that of rest of India, and therefore has demanded recognition for Nagaland as an independent state with a separate flag and constitution, since Independence. Even in Arunachal Pradesh which demographically marks an important section of the Sino-Indian border, the population largely comprises indigenous people who share their ethnolinguistic identities across the international border. For instance, three out of the four Mishmi clans – which is one of the twenty-six major ethnic communities of Arunachal Pradesh – live in India, while one is located on the Chinese side of the international border.

Consequently, the north-east has a diverse tradition of indigenous languages and oral/folk literatures which do not find expression in written archives. Continuous attempts on the part of the sovereign state of India to integrate and homogenise this diversity further add to the resistance claiming recognition for their subalternised identities. Indian English literature in the form of stories and poetry from the North-east register these unique features of their indigenous identities. With constant references to the oral folklores, myths and customs, these writings introduce into the domains of literature the lost voices of marginalised traditions. For instance, the works of the Naga poet Temsüla Ao represent the traditions and folklores of the Ao Naga community of Nagaland. In her collection of short stories titled *These Hills Called Home: Stories from a War Zone* (2005), Ao provides an alternative perspective to the mainstream nationalist narrative of Nagaland becoming an Indian state in 1963. These stories present a contrapuntal understanding of individual and collective trauma in a land which has been going through a continuous state of war for decades within the territorial demarcation of a nation state.

In her Preface to the volume, Ao declares her purpose: to 'revisit the lives of those people whose pain has so far gone unmentioned and unacknowledged' (ix). The technique of narration adheres to the longstanding practice of storytelling in oral literatures. While the story 'An Old Man Remembers' narrates the sense of futility and disillusionment of Sashi as his grandson asks him about his past, 'The Last Song' familiarises readers with the legend of Apenyo – a woman who was gang-raped by the army as she sang her last song which is still said to haunt the village. 'The Last Song', in fact, ushers in an eco-feminist perspective as the aggressive armed warfare sanctioned by the state is represented to be the masculinist domain while the brutalised woman becomes a metaphor for the land itself. Similarly, Ao's poetry is replete with references to the rich folk tradition of Nagaland and the subject for her poems permeate everything from the creation myths of the Ao Naga community (in poems such as 'The Stone-people from Lungterok') to the myth of the Ao Naga boatman who is believed to be transporting the souls of the dead from the land of the living to the land of the dead (in the poem 'Nowhere Boatman'). Written to reconstruct the lost histories of the indigenous people, the works of Temsüla Ao introduce a significant interruption in the otherwise smooth-flowing nationalist narrative of postcolonial history of India.

Another important instance of voicing resistance against the mainstream tendency of obliterating indigenous identities in the context of north-east India may be seen in the works of Mamang Dai, a renowned poet and short story writer from Arunachal

Pradesh. In her article titled 'On Creation Myths and Oral Narratives', Dai emphasises the importance of the oral traditions embedded in the folk cultures of the indigenous people and writes that one of the defining characteristics of these oral traditions is that their significance becomes prominent only as individuals grow up and look for their roots, their cultural identities. It is at this stage of self-realisation that these stories 'are not even perceived as stories anymore but as beliefs determining a way of life' (4). In her collection of short stories, *The Legends of Pensam*, Dai provides an insight into the lives and beliefs of the Adi people of the Siang valley which spans across Arunachal Pradesh and Tibet. The word *'pensam'* in the native language means 'in-between' or the 'middle ground'. Accordingly, the collection narrates stories of people whose existence is defined by the in-between spaces of myth and reality, as they experience their identities as caught between the traditional modes and the modern world.

Divided into four parts, *The Legends of Pensam* represents the flow of life of the villagers. The first part begins with the stories of the first generation of villagers. The second part narrates the stories of the time when a British administrative unit is set up in the village, leading to an intermingling of cultures. The third section traces the altered lives of the second generation of villagers, while the fourth shows a continuity of inheritance as the second generation people pass away gradually and the third and fourth generations take their place in the social set up. Collectively, the stories offer an insight into oral traditions and local beliefs, which, though they may sound incredible and other-worldly to the modern world steeped in the rationalist discourses of the West, define and shape the lives of the villagers. For instance, the first story, 'the boy who fell from the sky', is the story of a boy named Hoxo who fell from the sky and was brought to the village by Lutor. The villagers accept Hoxo unquestioningly, despite his apparently unbelievable origin, and Hoxo gradually grows old as an individual belonging to the community. These stories defy attempts at mainstream interpretations through the Western concepts of science and logic, and uphold a system of faith particular to this subaltern community hidden from the encroachments of the dominant discursive analyses.

The North-east is home to several small ethnic communities and each of them has their wealth of folk literature including stories, myths and legends. Sometimes, writers from the North-east retrieve from this wealth of oral literatures stories of historical warriors whose heroic contributions are unknown to mainstream nationalist historiography. One such work is *The Bronze Sword of Thengpakhri Tehsildar* by Indira Goswami (translated by Aruni Kashyap). Set in late-nineteenth-century Assam before the formation of the Indian National Congress, this historical novel narrates the story of a Bodo freedom fighter named Thengpakhri, believed to be the first woman revenue collector in British India. Living as a widow in a society where the educated Indians as well as the British administration were trying to address social evils such as sati and child marriage, Thengpakhri challenges the misogynist norms of patriarchy as she rides across the plains of the Bijni kingdom wearing a hat and carrying a sword, alongside the British officers. She is recreated by the novelist as an introspective character who speaks little, but her actions define her as a woman with a fiercely independent spirit and mind.

In the novel, Thengpakhri is represented as a character whose presence evokes respect from men as they see in her a woman who is far ahead of her times. Her contribution to the nationalist struggle emerges as she joins the underground struggle for independence and fights for the liberation of her people from the colonial rule. It is interesting to note that while Rani Lakshmibai pervades official historiography and nationalist struggle, Thengpakhri finds no mention in archived historical records. She lives in folklores, songs and stories of the Bodo community. The reason is quite obvious – Bundelkhand is an integral part of the Indian heartland when compared to the smaller kingdoms of the North-east. Moreover, Hindi is spoken by a comparatively larger section of the population than Bodo, which was added to the Eighth Schedule of the Constitution of India as an official language by the 92nd Constitutional Amendment Act in 2003. Goswami's novel, therefore, resurrects the figure of Thengpakhri as a subalternised Other from the oral traditions, and re-narrativises the forgotten contribution of the Bodo community to the Indian nationalist movement.

Of Kashmir

Any discussion of borderlands and subalternisation in India remains incomplete without a reference to Kashmir. In 'Democracy and Violence in India and Beyond', Ramachandra Guha traces a detailed history of the Indian attempts at the political territorialisation of Kashmir since 1947 and a continuous history of prolonged dominance. He notes how the Kashmiri youth 'rose in rebellion against these cumulative injustices' in 1989, and how their actions 'were endorsed by many ordinary Kashmiris' who called for '*azadi*, or freedom, from the Indian rule' (35). Historically, the discourse of subalternisation in Kashmir acquired a new dimension with the rise of 'Hindutva' in twentieth-century India. This new political formation sought to impose on the unique and hybrid Kashmiri identity, encapsulated in the term *kashmiriyat*, claims of integration to the Indian heartland, based on the facts that Kashmir had been ruled by a Hindu ruler, Hari Singh, before Independence, and that the population of Kashmir included the Hindu Kashmiri Pundits who had suffered unimaginable atrocities at the hands of Muslim insurgents. Such arguments overlooked the traditional hybridity of cultural confluences that had permeated the valleys of Kashmir since the thirteenth century, through its close ties with Persian political ideologies and Central Asian Sufi mystics, which had shaped the sense of identity of Kashmiri communities. The lives of Kashmiris came to be gradually subjected to the demands of submission based on postcolonial cartographic delineations.

Ananya Jahanara Kabir traces a cultural trajectory of how Kashmir has been romanticised through the camera and geopolitically transformed into a fetish of desire as 'paradise on earth'. Kabir writes that Kashmir 'as landscape has been subject to the camera's gaze like no other space in South Asia', tracing the origins of this exoticised gaze back to Samuel Bourne and John Burke in the 1860s (14). The result has been the development of what Kabir terms as 'cinepatriotism', which has pervaded the mainstream Indian nationalist imagination regarding the geospatiality of a desired fantastical territory called Kashmir, through repeated representations in popular culture and films.

Chitralekha Zutshi provides a detailed overview of research around Kashmir and Kashmir Studies through the post-Independence period to the present times in 'Whither Kashmir Studies?: A Review', and observes that though scholarship around Kashmir has come a long way since the decades after Indian Independence and the end of the twentieth century has seen a shift in perspective with more people-centric works, a lot remains to be done. Zutshi suggests 'a broadening of the scope of Kashmir Studies to include historical studies of the early, medieval and early modern periods' from the borderlands perspective in order to retrieve the lost episodes of Kashmir's regional history.

Indeed, the complexity and uniqueness of *kashmiriyat* reveals itself as one studies the historical development of Kashmiri literature and its diverse forms and content. One of the earliest works in Kashmiri literature is the *Mahanaya Prakasha* by Shiti Kanta, written in the thirteenth century. It is a philosophical treatise on Kashmiri Shaivism. However, it is Lal Ded or Lalleshwari who is considered to have brought the tenets of Kashmiri Shaivism closer to the people through her verses, called *Vakhs*, composed in the language of the common people. Dating back to the fourteenth century, Lal Ded is still considered as one of the most important spiritual poets in Kashmiri. Her *Vakhs* – generally four-line stanzas without a uniform rhyme scheme – preach the philosophy of unity between Hindus and Muslims, and are opposed to rituals and idol worship. For instance, in one of her *Vakhs*, she writes, 'God is everywhere, do not discriminate between the Hindu and the Muslim. If you are wise, try to know yourself and this is the only way to know God' (Choudhuri 19). Lal Ded's *Vakhs* were first collected and translated into English by George Abraham Grierson, and were published in 1920; and till date, they form the initial recitations in folk performances, as they survive in Kashmiri literature almost as allegories and parables from the past. Her tradition is carried forward by her disciple Nund Rishi.

The influence of Sufi thought and mysticism further enriched the Kashmiri language from the fourteenth century onwards. In the songs composed by Habba Khatoon in the fifteenth century, one finds the beginnings of the lyric tradition in Kasmiri literature. Her *Vachanas*, as they are called, are songs full of pathos and longing for her beloved, Yusuf Shah. These *Vachanas* are cherished till date, and they mark the beginning of a new form in Kashmiri literature. With the rapid infiltration of Persian words into the Kashmiri language at this stage, later Kashmiri literature in the nineteenth century saw the emergence of another important literary form called *Masnavi*. Introduced initially by Mumin Saab, it is, however, *Gulrez* by Maqbool Shah Kralawari which remains celebrated as the most famous *Masnavi* in Kashmiri literature, and it has been adapted for performance and translated repeatedly. Based on a Persian story, *Gulrez* is treated as a masterpiece of literature representing the theme of love and also bearing a spiritual message from early nineteenth century. The work is appreciated for its sweetness, melody and poetic spontaneity. When contemporary scholarship around Kashmir does not allude to this rich past as the source of the unique ethnolinguistic identity of the people, it is clear that such research is dominated by the political turmoil and violence.

While it is true that this violence forms an integral component of the lives of the people of Kashmir, denying them their voice and the right to self-determination, at the same time, it is important to acknowledge that the sense of identity for any region evolves as a part of an uninterrupted flow of multiple currents which cannot be defined or comprehended by a compartmentalised study of the political or commercial policies alone. This representation of the self shaped by multiple resonances may be found in the poetry of Agha Shahid Ali. Based in the United States after his journey through Kashmir and New Delhi, Ali's poetry expresses a nostalgic yearning for the valley he belongs to, especially in his volume of poems *The Country Without a Post Office* (1997), published as a reaction to the violence in Kashmir in the 1990s. In the Prologue to the volume, Ali refers to the songs of Habba Khatoon and in the context of 'mass rapes in the villages, towns left in cinders' imagines the people to be singing her songs which had then 'roused the people to frenzied opposition to Moghul rule' (2). Further, in his poem 'Farewell', Ali visualises how 'in the lake the arms of temples and mosques are

Extending the Boundaries 157

locked in each other's reflections', re-invoking the multi-religious, multicultural past of Kashmir and comments, 'They make a desolation and call it peace' (5).

It may be argued that Agha Shahid Ali was recreating nostalgic pictures of the land he had left behind and subjecting it to an outsider's gaze, moulded by the Western point of view. Yet what cannot be denied is his unique insider's understanding of the amalgamation and confluence of ideas that shapes the concept of *kashmiriyat*. Nida Sajid comments on how Ali's poetry constitutes a counter-discourse to the mainstream archives narrating Kashmir and 'gifts us a Kashmir accessible only to him in a voice partitioned into many selves navigating the ever-shifting borders of language and history' (91). Sajid equates the perspective adopted by Ali in his poetry about Kashmir with Gloria Anzaldúa's concept of the 'atravesado' in *Borderlands/La Frontera: The New Mestiza* (1987), to implicate the in-betweenness of a hyphenated identity who 'inhabits both an imaginary and a real borderland'; and in doing so, Sajid bridges the geo-temporal distance between the borderland perspectives with reference to Kashmir and Latin America (86).

Of Latin America

Being located on the borderland results in the inculcation of a double vision as the individual belongs to the nation and yet remains a marginalised Other. This Otherness or alienation may be experienced in terms of markers such as language, culture, race, caste, gender, religion, ethnicity, or any other component of identity which subjects the individual or group to liminality and leads to subjugation. In *Local Histories/Global Designs: Coloniality, Subaltern Knowledges and Border Thinking*, Walter Mignolo uses the term 'border thinking' to refer to 'knowledge from a subaltern perspective' which is 'conceived from the exterior borders of the modern/colonial world system' (13). According to Mignolo, 'border thinking' as an ideology seeks to retrieve the force and creativity of indigenous forms of knowledge subalternised during the colonial period, and therefore, offers a counter-discourse by interrogating the hegemonic systems of knowledge constituted by Western thought, modernity and reason. In the Latin American context, the Chicano or the Mexican American identity represents such indigenous population who have suffered sustained forms of racial and cultural subjugation at the hands of the white American society. This led to the Chicano Movement in the 1960s and seventies, inspired by the Black Power Movement of the African American community. As a result, the racial–political ideology of Black–Brown unity emerged as a response to white supremacy in twentieth-century America, aiming to end racial exploitation.

Literature offers an alternative archive documenting the utterances of the subjugated Other. One such work published during the Mexican American Civil Rights Movement is *Chicano* (1970) by Richard Vasquez. Through the description of the experiences of the Sandoval family after their relocation to the United States following the Mexican Revolution, the novel paints a picture of the social reality in America with reference to racial politics, injustice and discrimination. It portrays the journey of four generations of a Mexican American family and traces their social escalation from immigrant agricultural labourers to the first graduate from a business school in Los Angeles. Vasquez reveals the habitual homogenising tendencies of the Anglo-American society ignorant about the Chicano identity, through interpersonal relationships, such as that shared by Mariana – the daughter from the third generation of the Sandoval family – and her friend David who hails from the white American background. As Mariana reveals to David that her grandfather is illiterate, the shock expressed by him is emblematic of the complacent ignorance about the marginalised Other. Their interactions and conversations highlight the culture clashes and the nuances of racial discrimination. The question of legitimacy and acceptance of the Other is further problematised as David refuses to marry Mariana who is pregnant with his child. Vasquez, himself a representative of the Mexican American identity, further uses the voice of an omniscient narrator intercepting the dialogues between the characters in the novel in order to critique the socio-cultural and racist practices of discrimination. Immensely popular from the time of its publication, *Chicano* remains an important literary representation negotiating questions of borders, marginalisation, immigration, discrimination and urbanisation in the context of the Mexican American community.

Another important Latin American discourse on the Chicano perspective, from a feminist point of view, is provided by *Borderlands/ La Frontera: The New Mestiza*, by Gloria E. Anzaldúa. Published in 1987, this semi-autobiographical work, a blend of prose and poetry, problematises the perceived binaries between Latino and non-Latino existence. Juan-Bruce Novoa defines the Chicano identity as living 'in the space (not the hyphen) between' Mexican-American (27). Anzaldúa redefines *'mestizaje'*, i.e., the hybridity and multiplicity of the individual identity in the Chicano context, as that which permits discrimination but also allows the individual to develop transformative modes of thinking. In *Borderlands*, Anzaldua writes, 'This is my home / this thin edge of / barbwire' (25). What is unique to this work is that it explores the double marginalisation of the gendered Chicano and unravels a journey towards liberation. From mapping the territory of displacement along cartographic lines, Anzaldúa's text becomes a declaration of a feminist rebellion by the new mestiza reclaiming her body and sexuality, and demanding her freedom from patriarchal subjugation as also the larger oppressive forces of mainstream culture along the borderlines.

Even in terms of its language, *Borderlands* employs a unique structure of signs by switching between multiple linguistic codes – from English to Castilian Spanish to the North Mexican dialect. In her Preface to the first edition, Anzaldúa declares that this technique enables her to portray 'a new language – the language of the Borderlands', for here, 'at the juncture of cultures, languages cross-pollinate and are revitalized' (20). This inherent hybridity of identity – which is not only confined to language but also speaks for a hybrid cultural inheritance hyphenated by porous borders – is traced by the book, as the borderlands explored are not just geo-spatial borderlines, but also psychological, sexual and spiritual borderlands which are not restricted to any specific geographical region.

★★★

In *The Nation and Its Fragments*, Partha Chatterjee observes that 'the ethical domain of nationalism remains very much a contested terrain' (157). He explores the plural societies within a nation that constitute, and are also at the same time subsumed by, the hegemonic power of a unified nationalist narrative, with reference to the women, peasants and outcastes as communities comprising the nation. The centrality of the mainstream nationalist narrative in terms of discourse is, therefore, surrounded by multiple other narratives voicing the subalternised sections of the population. The borderlands perspective and the multiple worlds inhabiting the same cartographic demarcations can also be seen to be extensions of these peripheral narratives that provide contrapuntal perspectives on and interrogate the hegemonic location of the centre of nationalist discourse. In the first chapter of *The Argumentative Indian*, Amartya Sen observes that 'a defeated argument that refuses to be obliterated can remain very alive' (16). The peripheral voices of these subjugated communities, similarly, continue to resonate through dominant nationalist histories and assert their claim to legitimisation, despite a prolonged period of sustained postcolonial subalternisation.

REFERENCES

Ali, Agha Shahid. *The Country Without a Post Office*. Penguin Books, 2013.

Anzaldua, Gloria. *Borderlands/La Frontera: The New Mestiza*. Aunt Lute Books, 1999.

Ao, Temsüla. *These Hills Called Home: Stories from a War Zone*. Penguin books, 2005.

Chatterjee, Partha. *The Nation and Its Fragments: Colonial and Postcolonial Histories*. Princeton UP, 1993.

Chatterji, Suniti Kumar. '"Adivasi" Literatures of India: The Uncultivated "Adivasi" Languages'. *Indian Literature* 14.3 (1971): 5–42. JSTOR, <www.jstor.org/stable/23329913>.

Choudhuri, Indranath, ed. *Encyclopaedia of Indian Literature, Volume III*. Sahitya Akademi, 2014.

Dai, Mamang. 'On Creation Myths and Oral Narratives'. *India International Centre Quarterly* 32.2/3 (2005): 1–6. JSTOR, <www.jstor.org/stable/23005996>.

----. *The Legends of Pensam*. Penguin Books, 2006.

Dutta, Kumar Ajit. *Maranya charer itikatha*. Swarer Arale Sruti Prakashani, 2019.

Goswami, Indira. *The Bronze Sword of Thengpakhri Tehsildar*. Tr. Aruni Kashyap. Zubaan, 2013.

Guha, Ramachandra. 'Democracy and Violence in India and Beyond'. *Economic and Political Weekly* 48.14 (2013): 34–40. JSTOR, <www.jstor.org/stable/23527283>.

Guha, Ranajit. *Subaltern Studies II: Writings on South Asian History and Society*. Oxford UP, 1983.

Kabir, Ananya Jahanara. *Territory of Desire: Representing the Valley of Kashmir*. U of Minnesota P, 2009.

Ludden, David, ed. *Reading Subaltern Studies*. Permanent Black, 2002.

Manuel, George, and Michael Poslun. *The Fourth World: An Indian Reality*. Collier-Macmillan Canada, 1974.

Mignolo, Walter D. *Local Histories/Global Designs: Coloniality, Subaltern Knowledges, and Border Thinking*. Princeton UP, 2000. JSTOR, <www.jstor.org/stable/j.cttq94t0>.

Mitra, Amar. *Kumari megher desh chai*. Dey's Publisher, 2019.

Novoa, Juan-Bruce. 'The Space of Chicano Literature'. *De Colores* 1.4. Pajarito Press, 1975.

Pandey, Gyanendra. 'In Defense of the Fragment: Writing about Hindu–Muslim Riots in India Today'. *Representations* 37 (1992): 27–55. JSTOR, <www.jstor.org/stable/2928653>.

Rodríguez, Ileana, ed. *The Latin American Subaltern Studies Reader*. Duke UP, 2001.

Sajid, Nida. 'The Transnational Cartography of Agha Shahid Ali's Poetry'. *Rocky Mountain Review* 66 (2012): 85–92. JSTOR, <www.jstor.org/stable/rockmounrevi.66.85>.

Sen, Amartya. *The Argumentative Indian*. Penguin Books, 2006.

Singh, Amritjit, and Peter Schmidt. *Postcolonial Theory and the United States: Race, Ethnicity and Literature*. UP of Mississippi, 2000.

Vasquez, Richard. *Chicano*. Harper Collins, 2005.

Zutshi, Chitralekha. 'Whither Kashmir Studies?: A Review'. *Modern Asian Studies* 46.4 (2012): 1033–48. <www.jstor.org/stable/41478427>.

Archive, Goethe Institut, Kolkata: Indo Bangladesh Enclaves. <https://www.goethe.de/ins/in/en/sta/kol/pro/inm/cib.html>.

Chapter Nine

Reading Subalternity in Films

Since the exploration of subaltern subjectivity depends on alternative sources of historiography and documentation, the role of the arts, mainly literature and films, becomes one of great significance. In both the cases, the form and content merge to portray a certain sequence of plausible events which might have occurred in the life of a subaltern individual or community at a given point of time in history. These narratives can be read against the socio-historical axes of space and time in order to decode the subaltern utterance.

Detailed analyses of literary works and perspectives have been provided with reference to subalternity in the previous chapters. We will take up films in this chapter. Films, as a form of mass media, exercise great power on popular imagination, and reach a wider audience when compared to literature. The visual impact of a story narrated as spectacle, as also their ability to engage with audience who lack 'literacy', enables films to portray social realities and leave a deep impression on viewers.

FILMS AND REPRESENTATION OF THE SUBALTERN

As the very act of representation depends upon a narrative medium, the subject-position of the narrator needs careful analysis in order to comprehend the form of representation under scrutiny. While in the case of literature, the gaze of the narratorial voice is located within the text, in the case of films, it becomes imperative to understand the gaze of the camera, for the camera which portrays and substitutes the silent omniscient narrator of literature, invariably interprets facts and is hardly ever a neutral observer of people and events. Technically divided into the elements of diegesis and spectacle, films as a form of representation function through a duality of exposition – while diegesis offers the story, spectacle creates visual impact through identification or alienation, in turn leading to a spectrum of emotional responses. Films aiming at representing subalternity, more often than not, highlight the exploitation and suffering of the subjugated through the use of spectacle. In doing so, they foreground harsh social realities and violence which leaves a deep impression on the viewers. Since the Hindi-language film industry, or Bollywood, caters to a large section of population in India and worldwide, the examples of subaltern representations in films discussed in this chapter have been taken from Bollywood films.

CASTE AND CLASS IN FILMS

One of the important films voicing the angst of the subaltern caught in the perpetual system of social exploitation based on caste as well as class is Govind Nihalani's *Aakrosh* (1980). It depicts the story of Lahanya Bhiku, a peasant in rural Maharashtra who earns his living as a daily labourer, as he is subjected to ruthless exploitation by the able and the powerful. Bhiku belongs to an aboriginal community and lives in a small village. The film begins with the lighting of a funeral pyre as the convicted Bhiku has his handcuffs removed by a policeman to perform the last rites. It is gradually revealed that Bhiku has been charged with the murder of his wife, Nagi. The defence lawyer tries his best to get Bhiku to speak but cannot extract a single word from him. Bhiku remains silent as the court proceedings continue. Exposition occurs through episodes of flashback, where it is revealed to the audience that Bhiku represents the exploited class who are reduced to voicelessness and subjected to brutal forms of torture by the politically influential people and the rich landowners. It is further revealed that Bhiku's wife was raped and murdered by these influential men and their goons, in front of him. Almost silent throughout the length of the film, the violation of his individuality and human existence finds expression as Bhiku screams at the end of the film, after murdering his sister with a blow of the axe at the cremation of his father.

Bhiku's final act is his expression of helplessness, disgust and suppressed anger. At the cremation of his father, he sees his sister as the next possible target for the influential people of the village. His subject position as an individual subalternised through class as well as ethnicity, does not allow him to offer any security to her. By striking the blow at her, he strikes at the social power hierarchy which renders people like him and their families vulnerable to all sorts of sustained physical and psychological violence. The futility of systems of justice and legislature is revealed by the fact that Bhiku, despite being innocent, must remain a convict accused of a crime which has, in reality, been committed against him. The entire length of the judicial proceedings presented in the film becomes an absurd narrative, a metafiction, where the demarcation between the victim and the accused gets completely obliterated by practices of subalternisation. Bhiku becomes the victim of not just the crime he is convicted for, but also the social practice which construes such fictional narratives asserting power, and thereby, leading to the subjugation and exploitation of the downtrodden. The case against Bhiku presented in the court of law, therefore, becomes a mockery of law and order. The film bears the subtitle 'The Cry of the Wounded' in English. Bhiku's silence is representative of submission and trauma. His cry at the end of the film is the helpless outcry of the hapless subaltern. Based on a real incident which took place in Maharashtra in 1976, *Aakrosh* problematises not just the dynamics of subalternisation but also the entire constitutional idea of law and order, and justice.

Another important film depicting caste-based subalternisation is *Sadgati* (1981), directed by Satyajit Ray. Based on a story of the same name by Munshi Premchand, *Sadgati* reveals the plight of Dukhia, a tanner ('*chamaar*'). He lives in the 'untouchable' quarters of the village with his wife Jhuria and their daughter. The film begins with Dukhia, who has just recovered from a fever, cutting grass and instructing his wife and daughter to ensure proper hospitality for the village brahmin whom he is about to visit. Dukhia refuses to eat before leaving, fearing that he will be late and rushes to the brahmin's house to invite to him to his place in order to fix the date for his daughter's engagement. The brahmin declines to accompany him immediately, and orders Dukhia to sweep his courtyard, clear the warehouse and to chop wood. Weak and hungry, Dukhia completes the first two tasks, but unaccustomed to chopping wood, he is unable to split even a single piece of wood from the obstinate branch of a huge tree, which has been assigned to him. Frustrated, Dukhia strikes the bark of the tree in a state of frenzy with quick successive blows, and eventually dies. The brahmin, on hearing of Dukhia's death, goes to the *'chamaar'* quarters of the village and asks them to remove the corpse. Having been already informed by a narrator belonging to the same community who had witnessed Dukhia's plight and had even offered him tobacco for comfort, the tanners of the village refuse to take orders from the brahmin. He makes a hasty escape from the place, fearing resistance. It soon begins raining while Dukhia's corpse is left untouched, and his wife wails over his lifeless body. Late in the night, the brahmin himself drags the corpse by tying its foot to a hook, to a garbage dump, since he is forbidden to touch the lower castes. The film concludes with the cleansing rituals being performed by the brahmin, with the axe still firmly stuck in the obstinate piece of wood, as a reminiscence of the last blow struck by Dukhia.

As the brahmin chants *shlokas* from the *Garuda Purana* – one of the eighteen *Mahapuranas* of Hinduism dating back to the first millennium of the Common Era – the irony of the caste system is highlighted because the *shloka* being recited hails purity as a virtue embedded in any and every individual believing in God. Caste does not form a component of this utterance. However, the thoughtless ritualistic misappropriation of Hinduism for the perpetuation of the caste system which evolved in the brahminical era is highlighted by the film as an example of a Foucauldian discourse on power/knowledge. The scriptures and ancient texts in Hinduism which are cited as the foundation of the caste order and exploitation emerge as instruments appropriated by the people belonging to the higher castes, in order to exploit those belonging to the lower castes. The knowledge of these scriptures, restricted to the members of a particular caste, is transformed into weapons in the hands of the higher castes for ensuring stability of the caste hierarchy through exercise of knowledge as power and vice versa. The axe striking ineffective blows into the stubborn piece of wood emerges as a metaphor for futile individual attempts at negotiating with the age-old caste prejudices which have been socially implanted and nurtured to acquire enormous strength. The close shot of the axe stuck into the huge apathetic branch becomes a symbol of futile retaliation by the subjugated subaltern against the deep-rooted caste system.

Despite the oft-repeated political narratives of social and national progress during the last two decades and more, caste-based exploitation has not disappeared from the Indian society. A comparative analysis of the representation of the caste system in Bollywood films asserts this point further. A well-known example of a recent film on caste exploitation is *Article 15* (2019), directed by Anubhav Sinha. Based in a village in Uttar Pradesh, the film deals with the case of three Dalit girls who are reported missing. As the new police officer, Ayaan Ranjan, assumes charge at the police station, bodies of two of the three missing girls are found hanging from a tree one morning. The third girl, Pooja, is still missing. The investigating officer, Brahmadutt, informs Ayaan that the two girls who had been killed, shared a homosexual relationship. They had been caught in the act by their fathers and were thus punished in the form of 'honour killing'. As the film progresses, Ayaan discovers the strong grip of caste system on the villagers, including the officers of his police station whose activities and duties are determined by their caste. It is gradually revealed that the two girls, whose corpses had been discovered, were gang-raped for over two days and then murdered by hanging. They were engaged in construction of roads, employed by the son of the local minister; and their crime was to have asked their salary to be hiked by three rupees. Ayaan discovers that all the local representatives of political or state power – from the son of the local minister to the officers in his own police station – are involved in this crime, and that the doctor performing autopsy has been instructed to manipulate the reports as part of the conspiracy to dismiss the case.

The film addresses and problematises caste subjugation at multiple levels. According to Althusser's *Ideology and Ideological State Apparatuses*, the police or the military represent the Repressive State Apparatus (RSA) controlled by and functioning for the state. Though theoretically separate from the Ideological State Apparatuses (ISA) which are responsible for the ideological indoctrination of the subject, the RSAs are composed of individuals who are subjects indoctrinated to accept majoritarian mainstream standards of social and power hierarchies. The police officers at Ayaan's police station practising caste-based discrimination are therefore interpellated subjects of the caste system. Titled as *Article 15*, the film highlights the irony of these caste-ridden social practices by alluding to the Article 15 of the Constitution of India which declares, 'The state shall not discriminate against any citizen on grounds only of religion, race, caste, sex, place of birth or any of them'. When Ayaan pins a copy of Article 15 on the display board of his police station, the irony is further enhanced. As the fathers of the two murdered girls are framed for the crime, the hypocrisy of the legal institutions controlled by the state is interrogated. Those enjoying state-sanctioned power are presented as free to indulge in concentric cycles of victimisation, to strike a balance between the political and social evils, while upholding their own privileges. Further, the fact that the victims of sexual oppression are two young girls, highlights the double subjugation that women face within the caste order. While rape is an act of sexual violence against the gendered Other, the act of hanging them from the tree as spectacle is a message directed at the entire Dalit community, to remind them of their social position. However, as a part of mainstream media, the film, which is based on a real incident involving the death of two girls in Uttar Pradesh, offers a sense of justice by having three girls as victims and keeping the third one alive, so as to assure the viewers of the possibility of legal action against the accused.

GENDER IN FILMS

Just as the subject of caste exploitation has been variously explored in films, there have been several films which have dealt with gender as the basis of subalternisation. One of the important films representing gender discrimination is *Bazaar* (1982), directed by Sagar Sarhadi. Addressing the issue of 'bride buying' in India, *Bazaar* records the experiences of the protagonist Najma, as she witnesses young girls – some of them had just reached puberty – from poor families being sold to prospective grooms. Najma ends up as a victim as well as an active participant in this cycle of victimisation. As a woman from a respectable family in Hyderabad, Najma is told that she cannot be engaged in any kind of work which brings her to the public domain. Nonetheless, her mother advises her that to support her family, she might use her body in the darkness of the night so that it does not bring shame on her family. Najma enters into such a relationship with Akhtar Hussain who lures her with the promise of marriage should she accompany him and assist him to begin his own business. She relocates to Mumbai with Akhtar, and six years go by, but the promise of marriage remains unfulfilled. Rather, Akhtar soon convinces Najma that she should find a young bride for his client Shakir Khan who has come from the Gulf and has promised to lend money to Akhtar if he can find him a match. Najma is compelled to do so, despite knowing Shakir Khan to be an abusive husband in his previous marriage. She ends up finding a match for him in Shabnam – the love interest of her younger brother – but the girl eventually commits suicide on the night of the wedding.

Human trafficking as a social reality is represented in the form of multiple linked narratives in *Bazaar*. Through an exploration of the nuances and shades of inter-human relationships, the film engages in a sharp critique of patriarchy and marriage as a social institution. The body of the woman is transformed into a product and capitalised on by the social unit called family. Notably, the custom of bride buying is sanctioned by the families of the girls who are sold to prospective grooms at a mutually agreed price with the consent of their families. The mainstream narrative of 'honour' which is culturally construed around the female body by patriarchy is problematised by transforming the girls into sellable commodities. Similarly, the hegemonic construct of 'family' as the source of social security is interrogated by the film. Shabnam's suicide is the tragic assertion of the gendered subaltern's right to her own life and body. Najma is left to survive with the guilt of having been an instrument of exploitation at the hands of patriarchy. Her role becomes instrumental in understanding the perpetuation of this cycle of victimisation. Translating as 'the market', the title of the film highlights the commercial aspect related to this socially sanctioned process of human trafficking in the name of marriage. The worth of the woman is reduced to that of a sexual object whose sole purpose is to satisfy the desires of the man.

Another important film exploring the subject of gender-based subalternity is *Rudaali* (1993), directed by Kalpana Lajmi. Based on a story by Mahasweta Devi, *Rudaali* represents the life of a woman, Shanichari, belonging to a lower caste and located in a village in Rajasthan. Shanichari is named so because she was born on a Saturday – culturally, an ominous day – and hence, she is considered to be a harbinger of misfortunes. She soon loses her father, while her mother Peewli elopes to join a local folk theatre group, leaving her all by herself. At an early age, she is married off to a drunkard who dies due to cholera, and Shanichari is left with a son, Budhua, whom she loves deeply. She engages in different kinds of employment including at the local landlord's *haveli*, to earn a living. When Budhua grows up, he marries a young prostitute named Mungri, who soon aborts his child leading Budhua to abandon his home and his mother. The life of Shanichari is revealed in flashbacks as she narrates her story to Bhikni, who is a famous *rudaali* and has been summoned to mourn the local landlord after his death. The term *rudaali* has a cultural connotation. It refers to lower-caste women who are professional mourners hired to mourn the death of upper-caste and rich men in certain areas of Rajasthan. On the night of the landlord's death, Bhikni is had gone to the neighbouring village and news soon arrives that she had died of plague there. In her last moments, she had revealed that she was Peewli, the mother of Shanichari, and wanted this message to be conveyed to her. The film concludes with Shanichari – who had never shed a drop of tear at her own hardships throughout her life – assuming the role of a *rudaali* wailing aloud and mourning the death of the landlord.

Rudaali represents the plight of a subaltern, marginalised in terms of caste, class as well as gender. Deriving its title from a cultural practice, the story is rooted in rural India and narrates the plausible life of a subaltern. However, it is not just a monochromatic narrative of oppression. Shanichari might be living a miserable life, full of hardships, but when the blame for it is thrust upon her birth on a Saturday, she negates the popular belief by questioning the plight of other women whom she knows were born on other days of the week but whose lives are no better than hers. Her resistance against subjugation is represented as she stands firm against the slurs and abuse of the local priests and moneyed men. Similarly, her invincible spirit is revealed by her continuous switching from one job to another in order to assure sustenance for herself and her son. The commodification of tears in the film completely subverts the concept of grief. The likes of Shanichari who spend their lives in sorrow cannot afford to grieve. Their sorrows are regular incidents in the flow of life and must be assimilated in order to move on. Grieving and tears, by contrast, become leisurely activities associated with the privileged class and castes who can afford to arrange for a spectacle of loss. Shanichari represents the proletariat who resists violence and subjugation at various levels throughout the course of the film, and finally emerges as the trained subaltern labourer who sells her tears as her produce. Bhikni passes on to Shanichari not just the legacy of a traditional form of livelihood but the empowerment which will enable her to survive on her own terms in lieu of her service to the hypocritical privileged classes.

A comparatively recent film representing subalternisation on the basis of gender is *Bulbbul* (2020), directed by Anvita Dutt Guptan. Unlike *Bazaar* or *Rudaali*, here the female protagonist is not subjugated by class or caste. Based in nineteenth-century Bengal, *Bulbbul* narrates the story of a girl named Bulbul who was married off to the eldest son of a wealthy Thakur household at the age of five. She develops a close friendship with the youngest brother of the Thakur, Satya, who is almost her age. As they grow up, the Thakur becomes suspicious about Bulbul's relationship with Satya and arranges to send him to London for further education. His suspicion leads him to brutally assault Bulbul; and in a fit of rage, he mutilates her feet with iron bars. As a result, Bulbul's feet are inverted and she is unable to walk without the firm shoes prescribed by the local doctor, Sudip. However, during the course of her treatment, when Bulbul is completely confined to her bed, she is raped and strangled by the Thakur's twin brother who is mentally challenged. The film takes a supernatural turn hereafter as Bulbul is restored to life. Abandoned by her husband, she undergoes a transformation and lives to avenge the women who are wronged by their husbands in the village. Satya returns from London to find Bulbul as a powerful woman who runs the household in the absence of her husband. He is suspicious about her relationship with the doctor who comes to examine Bulbul's feet frequently and with whom she shares a friendly bond. The village is said to be haunted by a *chudail* – 'a female demon with inverted feet'. It ends with Satya discovering Bulbul to be the *chudail*, learning about the atrocities she had been subjected to and leaving the village fearing that he will also become a tyrant like his elder brother.

The film, despite catering to popular cinematic trends by incorporating a supernatural theme, raises important questions by linking the popular imagination about a female demon with a story of gender-based exploitation. While the facts of child marriage being prevalent in the nineteenth century are widely known, the film in focusing on the issues of mobility and agency of the woman raises certain thought-provoking issues. In the popular imagination, *chudail* or the female demon is characterised by inverted footmarks and is considered dangerous because of her power. By tracing Bulbul's evolution into a female demon, the film provides an alternative understanding of the misogynistic idea of monstrosity associated with the liberated female. Bulbul attains freedom only when she is rendered physically immobile by the violence inflicted upon her by her husband who is a representative of patriarchy. She is penalised by him for transgressing the accepted domains of gender codes through her camaraderie with Satya. Her death, though used with a cinematic purpose in the film, becomes her point of departure from mainstream patriarchal expectations, and her return to life signifies a re-birth. The new Bulbul to whom Satya returns is a fearless woman who exercises her power on the people residing within her territory. She acquires freedom of movement and her right to self-determination. Her choices are no longer informed by social considerations. She flouts the patriarchal codes of domestic confinement, and the film implies that it is perhaps in doing so that she emerges as the female demon – the monster who is feared by the patriarchy and whom it seeks to destroy. As Satya leaves the house, he also symbolically breaks the cycle of masculinist violence. While his physical departure is a choice he makes to end the legacy of traditional patriarchal values, his sympathy for Bulbul marks the emergence of a gender-sensitised individual leaving the decadent hierarchy of tyranny, to establish a new world.

NATIONALIST HISTORY IN FILMS

In terms of postcolonial history, the nationalist narratives of freedom represented in Bollywood films based on historical episodes aim at glorifying the mainstream archives, while also blending a presentist or even futuristic perspective into the events of the past. In *Philosophy of History,* M. C. Lemon identifies two kinds of approaches to history – Speculative and Analytic. He states that Speculative Philosophy of History stems from the impulse to make sense of history, to find meaning in it or at least an intelligible pattern. According to him, at the heart of this impulse is the desire to predict the future, and in many cases, to shape it. The period films from Bollywood based on episodes of the Indian nationalist movement exemplify this point. For instance, Ketan Mehta's *Mangal Pandey: The Rising* (2005) begins with the declaration, 'Where history meets proud folklore, there legends are born'. This statement hints at the blending of fact and fiction, and forms the basis for representation, re-interpretation and re-analysis of history, which the film attempts. In the context of the spread and influence that Indian diaspora has achieved in the twenty-first century, it is significant that the film had its world premiere at the Locarno Film Festival, in Switzerland. The film portrays in Mangal Pandey a character larger than life, rooting in him the historic potential of the tradition of individual heroism in India and shaping the historical events to form a spectacle of the 'First War of Indian Independence'.

Bearing little resemblance with the original historical character, Mehta's Mangal Pandey is a man who has had some initiation into the English language by virtue of his friendship with William Gordon, an English officer with the East India Company. He has a profound insight into the state of affairs in India, the ability to introspect and organise, a thirst for knowledge, and he can transcend social prejudices like caste and superstition in the interest of nationalism – all that is essential in the making of a hero, rendering him acceptable to the audience of the twenty-first century. History, here, is moulded to suit the taste and necessities of a trans-national audience. Historical facts across geo-spatial differences are merged to elevate Mangal Pandey, the martyr, to the level of a seer who prophesies the democratic form of governance in modern India when he criticises the narrow selfish interests and cowardice of the nawabs and rajahs of India in front of Azimullah and Tantia Tope. Resistance is here translated into power by immortalising the war-cry and spirit of Mangal Pandey, and merging it at the end with a clipping of Mohandas Karamchand Gandhi leading a mass-movement against the British in the twentieth century. In this manner, the legend of Mangal Pandey is reconstructed from the perspective of Speculative Philosophy of History, trying to establish within his name the futuristic vision of an independent nation.

DISABILITY IN FILMS

The subject of disability has also been variously approached by Bollywood films. While several mainstream films such as the *Golmaal: Fun Unlimited* series (2006, 2008, 2010, 2017 and 2021) use disability rather insensitively to provoke laughter, there are also many mainstream films portraying disability which approach the subject with sensitivity and compassion, such as *Black* (2005), *Paa* (2009), *My Name is Khan* (2010), *Taare Zameen Par* (2007) and *Barfi* (2012), to name a few. However, in the latter set of films, the approach towards disability mostly ranges from pity to admiration – a defined spectrum of the range of mainstream social responses towards disability. An early and memorable example of a sensible as well as sensitive approach towards disability may be seen in

Koshish (1972), written and directed by Gulzar. Translating as 'an effort', the title of the film depicts the central idea represented through it, as Haricharan and Aarti – the hearing-impaired and mute couple, who are the central characters of the film – make a relentless effort to survive through various hardships. While they confront social apathy and insensitivity on one hand, on the other, their disability makes them victims of mishaps which could have been avoided by the able-bodied. Nonetheless, their resistance is asserted by their refusal to surrender to the adversities. Despite the setbacks, they continue to live their lives according to their own convictions and eventually raise a son who is able to hear and speak. Their son finally marries a girl who is hearing-impaired and mute, like his parents. The film remains important in its non-judgmental vision of an inclusive society. Unlike the dominant modes of social response to disability even in the present times, *Koshish* does not adhere to common feelings of sympathy or admiration for the disabled. The tragedies and hardships faced by the main characters are presented as the trials and tribulations that any individual may face in their life. Haricharan and Aarti do not survive on people's sympathy. They improvise alternative models of survival within an ableist society and do not compromise on their right to self-determination or their dignity. Disability here becomes a thought-provoking subject. However, it is not portrayed as a limitation imposed on individual potentials, or projected as what Stella Young, the Australian disability activist, describes as 'inspirational porn', indicating the projection of disabled people accomplishing extraordinary feats in order to inspire the able-bodied.

★★★

Subalternity has had varied representations in Bollywood films. While most popular representations have sought to re-inscribe the dominant mainstream narratives related to the nation, caste, class and gender into the public psyche to ensure the role of media as an ISA which imparts stability to social hierarchies, there have also been some representations which have interrogated the dominant social discourse of power. Films like *Aakrosh*, *Sadgati*, *Bazaar* and *Rudaali* raise important questions about the normalised narratives of exploitation intrinsic to social orders. However, subjected to censorship by the state, these narratives do not emerge as realistic social critiques despite their best attempts. The microcosmic projection of the society is contrasted with the assurance of the existence of a larger society outside the cross-section portrayed in the cinematic narrative, which condemns the stagnancy and injustice represented in the film. In the process, the entire episode of subalternity depicted in the film becomes a distant projection of Otherness in a different space and time. Contemporaneity is denied. Rather, honour and recognition is conferred by state-sanctioned boards and agencies in the form of awards for makers or actors of these films as tokens of appreciation for their effort.

Representation in mainstream films adopts a different perspective. Either, like Ketan Mehta's *Mangal Pandey*, it endorses the mainstream narrative of heroism as an integral component of nationalism and reinforces the dominant nationalist narrative, or like *Article 15*, it reassures the viewer that social justice can be attained in the end (in the form of the third girl who is miraculously found alive and the upright police officer Ayaan Ranjan who defies the corrupt authorities to retrieve the truth). Films like *Bulbbul*, similarly, while addressing social concerns around oppression, relocate the incident as a factual referential to a distant time in the past, thereby facilitating a projection of social evils through a veil of alienation by restructuring the frame of time.

As a major form of popular culture, films shape public opinion. Shyam Benegal calls the influence of the Hindi film industry in India the 'hegemonistic order' and observes that 'popular Indian cinema is not the reality but the ideal'. Hence, most of these films tend to leave aside 'the harsh realities of caste, untouchability, gender discrimination and the varieties of feudal economic oppression that exist in traditional society' (22). Even while addressing these issues, they tend to shift the onus of exploitation or evil onto individual villainy so as to ascertain a sense of moral justice by the victory of the good over the evil at the end. Representation of subalternity in films mostly adopts a moderation of techniques ranging from individual villainy to critique of a system or society, which nonetheless, is removed from the present reality of the viewers. However, their significance lies in the fact that they introduce into the mainstream projections of social realities a counter-discourse with reference to subaltern subjectivity.

REFERENCES

Aakrosh. Dir. Govind Nihalani. Krishna Films Enterprises, 1980.

Althusser, Louis. 'Ideology and Ideological State Aparatuses'. *Literary Theory: An Introductory Reader*. Ed. Saugata Bhaduri and Simi Malhotra. Anthem Press, 2010.

Article 15. Dir. Anubhav Sinha. ZEE Studios, 2019.

Bazaar. Dir. Sagar Sarhadi. New Wave Productions, 1982.

Benegal, Shyam. 'Talkies, Movies, Cinema'. *India International Centre Quarterly* 37.1 (2010): 12–27. JSTOR, <www.jstor.org/stable/23006452>.

Bulbbul. Dir. Anvita Dutt Guptan. Clean Slate Filmz, 2020.

Koshish. Dir. Gulzar. Sippy Films, 1972.

Lemon, M. C. *Philosophy of History*. Routledge, 2003.

Mangal Pandey: The Rising. Dir. Ketan Mehta. Yashraj Films, 2005.

Rudaali. Dir. Kalpana Lajmi. NFDC, 1993.

Sadgati. Dir. Satyajit Ray. 1981. Doordarshan. <https://www.youtube.com/watch?v=gZSczRE8xNg>.

Stanford Encyvlopedia of Philosophy. <https://plato.stanford.edu/entries/foucault/>.

Glossary of Select Terms

Chokhamela: Fourteenth-century Bhakti poet and saint in Maharashtra who belonged to the Mahar caste. He was denied entry into temples due to his caste.

Cinepatriotism: The concept dates back to an eponymous article by Kenneth M. Gould (1928). It refers to the gamut of emotions generated in the viewers by cinema based on historical facts, which unconsciously or deliberately reinforce popular prejudices and notions.

Dadu Dayal: Sixteenth-century saint–poet who rejected caste restrictions and denied the authority of the Vedas. He inspired the formation of a new sect called Dadu Panth.

Dharmashastra: A collection of Sanskrit texts dating back to 600–200 BCE. They are said to provide codes of conduct and moral principles for Hinduism.

Eknath: Sixteenth-century Bhakti poet and saint based in Maharashtra who opposed the caste system and religion-based discrimination practised by orthodox brahmins.

First Wave Feminism: The initial phase of feminism in the nineteenth and early-twentieth century, which advocated social and political equality for women.

Garuda Purana: An important religious text of Vaishnavism which centres around lord Vishnu. Originally composed in Sanskrit, it dates back to the first millennium BCE. However, as is common with ancient texts, the original text of Garuda Purana too has expanded to include several interpolations across the ages. The subjects addressed in the text include topics related to life and living, rituals related to worship and forms of ethics, virtue and conduct.

Hinduism: A complex ancient religion based on several systems of philosophies, doctrines and rituals. The term Hinduism was, however, coined by British writers in the nineteenth century to refer to the branch of Indian religion followed by the Hindus.

Hindutva: A term which originated in 1923, and is attributed to Vinayak Damodar Savarkar, for defining 'Hindu-ness'. It is a political term seeking to define India on the basis of Hindu values. It forms the foundation of the vision and doctrines of Hindu nationalism or Hindu nationalist ideology.

Hybridity: In postcolonial studies, the term 'hybridity' is a recurrent concept. It is associated with the works of Homi K. Bhabha. It refers to the interdependence and intermingling of Eastern and Western concepts in colonial and postcolonial literatures. By negating binaristic thinking, hybridity offers an 'in-between space' which carries the meaning of culture. In doing so, it provides the space to destabilise dominant power hierarchies and explore alternative subject positions.

Ideological State Apparatus and Repressive State Apparatus: In 'Ideology and Ideological State Apparatuses' (1970), Louis Althusser observes that the state exercises its power over its subjects through the use of Ideological State Apparatus (ISA) and Repressive State Apparatus (RSA). The ISAs function through silent ideological indoctrination of the subjects and form part of the private domain. Examples of ISA include units such as the family, educational institutions, religious institutions, media, literature, arts, etc. The RSAs, on the other hand, function through violence and form part of the public domain. Examples of RSAs include the government, administration, army, police, etc.

Kabir Das: Fourteenth-century mystic poet based in Varanasi. According to the legends, Kabir was born to a Hindu woman and raised by a Muslim weaver. His life, songs and poetry preach the message of harmony and oppose orthodox ritualistic practices.

***Loka* and *Shastra* in Indian Literature:** *Loka* refers to folk/popular traditions, while *Shastra* refers to the classical tradition in Indian literature.

Manusmriti: An ancient Dharmashastra considered as an authoritative treatise on Hinduism. It is attributed to the mythical first man and law-giver Manu and dates back to circa 100 CE. It is said to uphold the caste system and advocate the subjugation of lower castes and women. Babasaheb Bhimrao Ambedkar had famously burnt the *Manusmriti* at the Mahad convention in 1927.

National Federation of Dalit Women: It is a non-governmental organisation founded by Ruth Manorama in 1995 to promote and fight for the rights of Dalit women.

Patidars: Landowners and agrarian caste based in Gujarat. They claim to be descendants of Lord Rama, the Hindu deity. The caste is further divided into several subcastes, such as Anjanas, Kadavas and Levas.

Second Wave Feminism: It refers to the phase of feminist discourses dating back to the 1960s which critiqued institutions of patriarchy and the cultural practices prevalent in society.

Seven Sister States: A popular term used to collectively refer to the states of Assam, Arunachal Pradesh, Tripura, Manipur, Mizoram, Meghalaya and Nagaland. The term was coined after the constitution of the North Eastern Council in 1971 and popularised by the journalist Jyoti Prasad Saikia who also published a book titled *The Land of Seven Sisters* (1976). Sikkim became the eighth state to be included among the North Eastern States of India in 2002.

Further Reading

Amin, Shahid. *Event, Metaphor, Memory: Chauri Chaura 1922–1992*. Oxford UP, 1995.

Beverley, John. *Subalternity and Representation: Arguments in Cultural Theory*. Duke UP, 1999.

Bhowal, Sanatan. *The Subaltern Speaks: Truth and Ethics in Mahasweta Devi's Fiction on Tribals*. Orient BlackSwan, 2016.

Bonnerjee, Samraghni, ed. *Subaltern Women's Narratives: Strident Voices, Dissenting Bodies*. Routledge, 2020.

Chakrabarty, Dipesh. *The Calling of History*. Permanent Black, 2015.

Chatterjee, Partha. *Empire and Nation: Selected Essays*. Columbia UP, 2010.

----. *Lineages of Political Society: Studies in Postcolonial Democracy*. Permanent Black, 2011.

Chaturvedi, Vinayak, ed. *Mapping Subaltern Studies and the Postcolonial*. Verso, 2000.

Chowdhury, Debdutta. *Identity and Experience at the India–Bangladesh Border: The Crisis of Belonging*. Routledge, 2018.

Gokulsing, K. Moti, and Wimal Dissanayake, ed. *Routledge Handbook of Indian Cinemas*. Routledge, 2013.

Guha, Ranajit, ed. *A Subaltern Studies Reader 1986–1995*. Oxford UP, 2000.

Gupta, Sonya Surabhi, ed. *Subalternities in India and Latin America: Dalit Autobiographies and the Testimonio*. Routledge India, 2021.

Hunt, Sarah Beth. *Hindi Dalit Literature and the Politics of Representation*. Routledge, 2014.

Kumar, Raj. *Dalit Literature and Criticism*. Orient BlackSwan, 2019.

Mayaram, Shail, M. S. S. Pandian, and Ajay Skaria, ed. *Subaltern Studies XII: Muslims, Dalits and the Fabrications of History*. Permanent Black, 2005.

Mocherla, Ashok Kumar. *Dalit Christians in South India: Caste, Ideology and Lived Religion*. Routledge, 2021.

Narayan, Badri. *The Making of the Dalit Public in North India: Uttar Pradesh 1950–Present*. Oxford UP, 2011.

Pandey, Gyanendra, ed. *Subalternity and Difference: Investigations from the North and South*. Routledge, 2011.

----, ed. *Subaltern Citizens and their Histories: Investigations from India and the USA*. Routledge, 2010.

Raina, Trilokinath. *A History of Kashmiri Literature*. Sahitya Akademi, 2002.

Sanyal, Srija, ed. *Gender, Sexuality and Indian Cinema: Queer Visuals*. Cambridge Scholars Publishing, 2023.

Sati, Someshwar, and G. J. V. Prasad, ed. *Disability in Translation: The Indian Experience*. Routledge, 2020.

Sati, Someshwar, G. J. V. Prasad, and Ritwick Bhattacharjee, ed. *Reclaiming the Disabled Subject: Representing Disability in Short Fiction*. Bloomsbury India, 2022.

Zutshi, Chitralekha. *Kashmir's Contested Pasts: Narratives, Geographies and the Historical Imagination*. Oxford UP, 2014.

----, ed. *Kashmir: History, Politics, Representation*. Cambridge UP, 2018.

Other books in the series

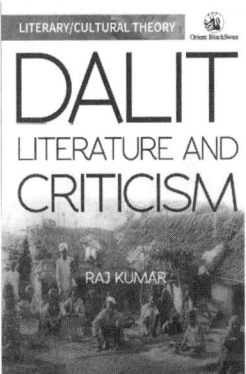

For more information, visit www.orientblackswan.com

Other books in the series

For more information, visit www.orientblackswan.com